VIRGINIA GENEALOGY

A Guide to Resources in the

University of Virginia Library

Virginia Genealogy

A GUIDE to RESOURCES

in the

University of Virginia Library

University Press of Virginia
Charlottesville

THE UNIVERSITY PRESS OF VIRGINIA
Copyright © 1983 by the Rector and Visitors
of the University of Virginia

First published 1983

Front cover: "Tree of Kinship" by Henricus de Segusio, Augsburg, Germany, 1477
(New York Public Library)

Back cover: Berkeley Family Bible (Manuscripts Department, University of Virginia)

Library of Congress Cataloging in Publication Data

University of Virginia. Library.
  Virginia genealogy.

  Includes index.
  1. Virginia—Genealogy—Bibliography—Catalogs.
2. Genealogy—Bibliography—Catalogs.   3. University
of Virginia. Library—Catalogs.   I. University of
Virginia. Library. Reference Dept.   II. Title.
Z1345.U57   1982   [F225]   016.929'1'0720755   82-8470
ISBN 0-8139-0958-9   AACR2

Printed in the United States of America

For Mabel Apple Talley

CONTENTS

PREFACE

This is a revision of our earlier guide, issued in 1977, and was the brainchild of Kendon Stubbs, my predecessor as Reference Librarian. Compilation and editing of the first edition was largely the work of Linda Bullock, Patricia Potter, and Raymond A. English, all formerly of the Reference staff. The present work has been through so many hands, it seems only appropriate to give authorship credit to the entire department.

Particular acknowledgments for their invaluable aid should be given to Clinton Sisson, Mary Topping, and Linda Wibert of the Alderman staff and innumerable library patrons who have made helpful suggestions over the years concerning this guide.

ROGER LEACHMAN
Director of Reference Services

VIRGINIA GENEALOGY

A Guide to Resources in the

University of Virginia Library

INTRODUCTION

The University of Virginia has a large number of genealogical sources among its holdings, including what must be considered one of the foremost collections dealing with Virginia genealogy. These materials—general guides and bibliographies, printed records, and manuscript sources—are scattered throughout the library system in the Reference Department, Rare Books Department, Manuscripts Department, the general stacks, and various branch libraries. This guide has been prepared in an attempt to make these sources more readily available to the genealogical researcher, whose time is often limited. We have not attempted to itemize all or even most of the genealogical materials in the library but have listed the basic sources that most of our researchers will need to locate. The bibliographies and materials listed in this guide can be used to identify further sources not mentioned here.

Although the bulk of our guide deals with sources for Virginia genealogies, the reader will find sections on genealogical research in general, on foreign genealogical sources, and on United States genealogy.

Following each item in the text is the library location symbol (see Location Symbols) and the Library of Congress call number. The inclusion of the latter may prove useful to the researcher attempting to use this guide with the collection of another library, although he must be cautioned that not all research libraries follow Library of Congress cataloging in all particulars. When there is occasion to doubt, the card catalog should be consulted.

To aid long-distance researchers, the University of Virginia Library's Interlibrary Loan section can fill requests placed through one's local library. However, manuscripts, reference books, and rare books cannot be sent on interlibrary loan. If photocopies of specific pages in a specific book are required, the Printing Services Department in Alderman Library fills such requests.

Other Virginia libraries that have large genealogical collections are:

Virginia State Library
12th & Capital Streets
Richmond, Virginia 23219

E. G. Swem Library
College of William and Mary
Williamsburg, Virginia 23185

Virginia Historical Society
428 North Boulevard
Richmond, Virginia 23221

Patrons interested in Charlottesville/Albemarle County genealogy may wish to visit or correspond with the Albemarle County Historical Society, Inc., 220 Court Square, Charlottesville, Virginia 22901.

LOCATION SYMBOLS

Film	Microform Room, 3d Floor, Alderman Library
Fine Arts	Fiske Kimball Fine Arts Library, Campbell Hall
Law Library	Law School Library, North Grounds
Mss.	Manuscripts Department, 2d Floor, Alderman Library
Health Sci.	Claude Moore Health Sciences Library
Pub. Docs.	Public Documents, 3d Floor, Alderman Library
Rare Book Coll.	Rare Books Department, 2d Floor, Alderman Library
Ref.	Reference Room, 4th Floor, Alderman Library
Sci. Tech.	Science/Technology Information Center, Clark Hall
Stacks	General stacks, Alderman Library

I.   GENERAL AIDS

Research Manuals—General

Patrons without experience or training in genealogical research should begin by consulting one or more of the following manuals, most of which are available in the Reference Room.

American Society of Genealogists. *Genealogical Research Methods and Sources*. Washington, D.C.: American Society of Genealogists, 1960. 2 vols.   Ref. CS16.A5
Excellent explanation of the use of public and institutional records. National, state, and regional chapters provide detailed information on the primary and secondary sources vital to genealogical research in each area and include descriptions of the archival material available. Pages 212–20 (vol. 1) cover genealogical research in Virginia.

Bennett, Archibald F. *A Guide for Genealogical Research*. Salt Lake City: Genealogical Society of the Church of Jesus Christ of the Latter-Day Saints, 1951.   Mss. CS16.B4 1951
Contains several useful appendixes, including foreign genealogical terms, legal terms, and date conversion tables from the Julian to the Gregorian calendar.

Cache Genealogical Library. *Handbook for Genealogical Correspondence*. Salt Lake City: Bookcraft, 1965.
                    Ref. CS16.C3 1964
Listing, by state, of names and addresses of libraries, archives, historical societies, and American church historical societies and archives that have genealogical holdings. There is also a list of genealogical publications that publish advertisements for genealogical inquiries.

Doane, Gilbert H., and James B. Bell. *Searching for Your Ancestors: The How and Why of Genealogy*. 5th ed. Minneapolis: University of Minnesota Press, 1980.   Ref. CS16.D6 1980
A standard account. Latest revision added chapters on "Ethnic Origins" and "Bridging the Seas." 4th edition (1973) included "Bibliography of Lists, Registers, Rolls, and Rosters of Revolutionary War Soldiers," omitted in this edition.

Greenwood, Val D. *The Researcher's Guide to American Genealogy.*
Baltimore: Genealogical Publishing Co., 1973.

Ref. CS47.G73

"Part I of this book deals with the basic principles of genealogical research as they apply to American ancestral problems
and Part II deals exclusively with those records in which the
student will do most of his research."

Helmbold, F. Wilbur. *Tracing Your Ancestry: A Step-by-Step Guide
to Researching Your Family History.* Birmingham, Ala.: Ox-
moor House, 1976.   Ref. CS16.H4
Concisely outlines proper search methods, record keeping,
organizing files, etc. Well suited for beginning researchers.
Bibliography of recommended sources.

Jaussi, Laureen Richardson and Gloria D. Chaston. *Fundamentals
of Genealogical Research.* 3d ed. Salt Lake City: Deseret Book
Co., 1977.   Ref. CS16.J38 1977
Basically formulated as a textbook, this is one of the most
useful manuals available. Details genealogical practices thor-
oughly and concisely, employing many helpful examples,
sample charts, etc. Emphasizes Latter Day Saints (Mormon)
practices, including an informative chapter on that church's
Computer File Index.

Jones, Vincent L. *Genealogical Research: A Jurisdictional Approach.*
Rev. ed. Salt Lake City: Genealogical Copy Service, 1972.

Mss. CS9.J63 1972

Emphasis placed upon the jurisdictional (or place of legal
residence) approach to genealogical research.

Lackey, Richard S. *Cite Your Sources: A Manual for Documenting
Family Histories and Genealogical Records.* New Orleans: Po-
lyanthos, 1980.   Ref. CS16.L34
A style manual for genealogical researchers, attempting to
provide "an uncomplicated, yet academically acceptable
guide to basic citations."

Parker, J. Carlyle. *Library Service for Genealogists.* Detroit: Gale
Research Company, 1981.   Ref. Z5313.U5P37

Intended primarily for librarians administering genealogical collections and services, this is nevertheless of great value to the general genealogical researcher.

Pine, Leslie G. *The Genealogist's Encyclopedia*. New York: Weybright and Talley, 1969.   Stacks. CS9.P48 1969b
A simplified guide, this book outlines record searching. It is especially helpful in its explanation of European records. Part II deals with heraldry, Part III with the clan system. Included are a heraldic glossary, a general glossary, and an index.

Stevenson, Noel C. *Search and Research: The Researcher's Handbook*. Whittier, Calif.: Western Printing Co., 1951.
                                   Ref. Z5313.U5S8 1951
A good beginner's handbook. Includes sources for genealogical information in the United States, United Kingdom, Ireland, and Canada as well as a directory of family associations.

Research Manuals—Ethnic

Interest in genealogical research once seemed to be relatively confined to the descendants of the first wave of settlers to arrive in this country, i.e., to "Anglo-Saxons"; therefore many genealogical research manuals concentrated on such emigration, to the neglect of other ethnic groups. The popularity of *Roots,* both as a book and a television miniseries, heightened the genealogical interest not only of Black Americans but of many other Americans of varied ethnic heritages.

Guides to research formulated for particular ethnic or religious groups may be located by consulting the subject card catalog under the name of the group or nationality (e.g., "Afro-Americans—Genealogy," "German-Americans—Genealogy").

The following are a few such research aids.

Blockson, Charles L, and Ron Fry. *Black Genealogy*. Englewood Cliffs, N.J.: Prentice-Hall, 1977.   Ref. CS21.B55
Best of the available guides to Afro-American genealogical research.

Jensen, Larry O. *A Genealogical Handbook of German Research*. Rev. ed. Pleasant Grove, Utah: Jensen, 1978.
Stacks. CS614.J46 1978

Miller, Olga K. ed. *Genealogical Research for Czech and Slovak Americans*. Detroit: Gale Research Company, 1978.
Ref. CS524.M54
Covers genealogical research in Czechoslovakia, archives here and abroad, Czech and Slovak names, etc. Slovaks not as comprehensively treated as Czechs.

Rottenberg, Dan. *Finding Our Fathers: A Guidebook to Jewish Genealogy*. New York: Random House, 1977. Ref. CS21.R58
A pioneering work; however, lack of index and heavy reliance on narrative limit its usefulness.

Smith, Clifford Neal, and Anna Piszczan-Czaja Smith. *Encyclopedia of German-American Genealogical Research*. New York: R. R. Bowker Company, 1976. Ref. E184.G3S66
More comprehensive than Jensen (above).

Bibliographies and Indexes

Genealogical bibliographies and indexes can aid the researcher in determining whether a family history has already been compiled, direct the genealogist to important and informative secondary sources, and provide shortcuts to locating and using primary record sources such as parish registers, deeds, and wills. Such bibliographies and indexes should be among the first sources consulted in any genealogical search.

The reader is urged to consult chapters II, III, and IV of this guide for listings of bibliographies and indexes that are specifically related to British and continental European genealogy, American genealogy, and Virginia genealogy.

Two of the major repositories of genealogical material are the Library of Congress and the Newberry Library in Chicago. Consulting the published catalogs of their genealogical holdings is an important beginning in genealogical research.

The Genealogical Index of the Newberry Library. Boston: G. K. Hall, 1960. 4 vols. Ref. CS44.N42 1960

This index is arranged by surname and, within surname categories, by state; thus it is possible to differentiate the Browns of Massachusetts from the Browns of Kentucky. Although all of the works included in the index refer only to the Newberry Library's collection of genealogical material, the index is useful in identifying titles that may be owned by other libraries.

U.S. Library of Congress. *Genealogies in the Library of Congress: A Bibliography.* Ed. Marion J. Kaminkow. Baltimore: Magna Charta Book Co., 1972. 2 vols.   Ref. Z5319.U53

Supplement, 1972–1976. Baltimore: Magna Charta, 1977.   Ref. Z5319.U53 Suppl. 1972–76
A listing of genealogical books and related materials in the collection of the Library of Congress. The arrangement is alphabetical by family name, and the volumes are cross-referenced.

The reader should note that genealogical material in the Library of Congress does not circulate and cannot be borrowed through interlibrary loan. Order forms for photocopies may be obtained from the Photoduplication Service Department at the Library of Congress. The Reference Room in the Alderman Library can furnish additional information about the hours of public service at the Library of Congress.

Biographical Dictionaries

Chapters II, III, and IV of this guide list American, British, and Virginia biographical dictionaries. Genealogists interested in historical biographical dictionaries for other countries should consult the subject card catalog under the name of the country, for example, "Germany—Biography."

The three sources below are basically "finding lists," that is, they refer the user to specialized biographical dictionaries which may provide specific information on the subject.

Hyamson, Albert M. *A Dictionary of Universal Biography of All Ages and All Peoples.* 2d ed. Reprint. London: Routledge and Kegan Paul, 1962.   Ref. CT103.H9 1962

An index to twenty-four of the most comprehensive biographical dictionaries and encyclopedias, including the Belgian, German, Italian, French, and Australian national biographical dictionaries. However, the *Dictionary of American Biography* and the *Dictionary of National Biography* are the only dictionaries that are completely indexed. Entries are arranged alphabetically by name, include birth and death dates and occupations, and refer the user to the appropriate dictionary source where additional information can be found.

Lobies, Jean Pierre, ed. *Index Bio-Bibliographicus Notorum Hominum*. Osnabrück: Biblio Verlag, 1974–   (In progress.)
Ref. Z5301.I5

A name index to the works included in Slocum (below). Part C, the "Corpus Alphabeticum," lists personal names, birth and death dates when known, occupation, and an item number which is keyed to the companion volume, "Liste der Werke," Part B. The "Liste der Werke" supplies a complete bibliographic citation to a source of biographical information on the subject. When finished, the *Index Bio-Bibliographicus* will be a multivolume set. Currently the work is only complete for those personal names from A through Brown, Robert.

Slocum, Robert B. *Biographical Dictionaries and Related Works*. Detroit: Gale Research Company, 1967.
Ref. Z5301.S55 1967

——. First Supplement. Detroit: Gale Research Company, 1972.   Ref. Z5301.S55 1967. Suppl.

——. Second Supplement. Detroit: Gale Research Company, 1978.   Ref. Z501.S55 1967. Suppl. 2
A bibliography of approximately 4,800 collective biographies, biobibliographies, selected genealogical works, historical and specialized dictionaries, and many other biographical sources. The arrangement, in three sections, is universal biography, foreign and U.S. biography by area, and foreign and U.S. national biography by vocation. The two supplements add 3,400 and 3,800 entries, respectively, to the bibliography. All volumes have author, title, and subject indexes.

Surname Dictionaries

Surname dictionaries can provide the genealogist with a solid foundation for further research. They often supply such useful information as variant spellings, descriptions of the origins of family names, nationality, and probably geographic locations of these names. The following is a basic list of surname dictionaries available in the Alderman Library. Patrons are urged to consult the subject catalog for additional material, which can be traced under the entry "Names, Personal" (e.g., "Names, Personal—Arabic."

Barber, Henry. *British Family Names, Their Origin and Meaning, with Lists of Scandinavian, Frisian, Anglo-Saxon, and Norman Names.* 2d ed., enlarged. London: Elliot Stock, 1903.
>Ref. CS2051.B29 1903

Includes over 10,000 names as well as lists of landholders, tenants, and undertenants listed in the Domesday Book.

Brechenmacher, Josef Karlmann. *Etymologisches Wörterbuch der Deutschen Familiennamen.* 2d ed. Limburg an der Lahn: C. A. Starke-Verlag, 1957–63. 2 vols.
>Ref. PF3576.B64 1957 (also in Stacks)

The most comprehensive dictionary of German family names, including more than 28,500 entries.

Dauzat, Albert. *Dictionnaire étymologique des noms de famille et prénoms de France.* Paris: Larousse, 1951.
>Ref. CS2691.D3 1951

Explains French surnames, given names, and geographic names; lists variant spellings.

Reaney, P. H. *A Dictionary of British Surnames.* 2d ed. London: Routledge and Kegan Paul, 1976.
>Ref. CS2505.R39 1976

Meanings and origins of British surnames with historical references to original uses. Variants given.

Sims, Clifford Stanley. *The Origin and Signification of Scottish Surnames, with a Vocabulary of Christian Names.* Albany, 1862; Baltimore: Genealogical Publishing Co., 1968.
>Ref. CS2435.S5 1968

Short annotations explaining meanings of Scottish surnames.

Smith, Elsdon C. *American Surnames*. Philadelphia: Chilton Book
  Co., 1969.   Ref. CS2485.S5 1969
  Discusses origins and classifications of names in general.

———. *New Dictionary of American Family Names*. New York: Har-
  per and Row, 1973.   Ref. CS2481.S55 1973
  Lists most common American surnames, particularly those of
  European origin. Provides brief descriptions of origin of
  name and designates nationality.

Heraldry

The art and science of heraldry can be of interest and importance
to the genealogist dealing with noble or landed families. Many of
the sources below can also be helpful in explaining and interpret-
ing the crests, arms, seals, and mottoes that are associated with cities, states, organizations, and businesses.
  The selection that follows includes most of the major sources of
heraldic information for Great Britain, Scotland, Ireland, and the
United States as well as the standard work on continental European armory.

Bolton, Charles Knowles. *Bolton's American Armory*. Boston:
  F. W. Faxon Company, 1927.   Ref. CR1209.B6 1927
  Register of the coats of arms that have been in use in the
  United States from colonial times to the present. The author
  disclaims authenticity of any of the coats of arms listed.

Boutell, Charles. *Heraldry, Ancient and Modern*. Rev. ed. Ed. S. T.
  Aveling. London: W. W. Gibbings, 1892.
                                      Ref. CR21.B67 1892
  History of the development of the various graphic elements
  of heraldic art. Includes chapters on seals, coins, and flags.
  Contains 488 clear illustrations. Glossary in chapter XIV;
  well indexed.

Burke, Sir John Bernard. *The General Armory of England, Scotland,
  Ireland, and Wales; Comprising a Registry of Armorial Bearings
  from the Earliest to the Present Time*. London: Harrison,
  1884; Baltimore: Genealogical Publishing Co., 1962.
                                      Ref. CR1619.B73 1962

Contains descriptions of over 60,000 coats of arms including "Noblemen and Gentlemen of the British Empire, and the various Coats that are to be seen in churches and family mansions, together with those traceable on Seals, Deeds, Wills, and Monumental remains." Except for royal arms there are no illustrations.

Crozier, William Armstrong. *A Registry of American Families Entitled to Coat Armor.* New York: Genealogical Association, 1904.   Ref. CR1209.C8
"Includes the known armigerous families of all the States in the Union . . . including not only the arms of persons of British ancestry, but of those whose ancestors came from Continental Europe." The arrangement is alphabetical by surname.

Crozier, William Armstrong, ed. *Virginia Heraldica; Being a Registry of Virginia Gentry Entitled to Coat Armor with Genealogical Notes of the Families.* New York: The Genealogical Association, 1908.   Ref. F221.V75 v.5 1908
Descriptions of the arms, crests, and mottoes of various Virginia families. Each entry includes a brief genealogy. The arrangement of the book is very poor, and there are no bibliographic references for the genealogies; however, there is an index at the end of the volume.

Elvin, C. N. *A Handbook of Mottoes, Borne by the Nobility, Gentry, Cities, Public Companies, etc.* London: Boil and Daldy, 1860; Detroit: Gale Research Co., 1971.
                                                    Ref. CR75.G7E5 1971
Arranged alphabetically by first letter in the motto, this volume provides an English translation of each motto and identifies its source.

Fairbairn, James. *Fairbairn's Crests of the Leading Families in Great Britain and Ireland.* New York, 1911; Baltimore: Genealogical Publishing Co., 1963. 2 vols. in 1.
                                                    Ref. CR57.G7F2 1963
The most complete collection of crests and mottoes; over 30,000 names arranged alphabetically, with descriptions of crests and cross-references to the plates that illustrate them.

Motto section is arranged alphabetically by mottoes and lists an English translation for each motto as well as the family or families using them.

Fox-Davies, Arthur Charles. *Armorial Families*. Edinburgh: T. C. & E. C. Jack, 1895.   Stacks. CR1619.F7 1895
Alphabetical arrangement by family name; provides biographical information, description of the arms, crest, and motto.

Franklyn, Julian, and John Tanner. *An Encyclopaedic Dictionary of Heraldry*. Oxford: Pergamon Press, 1970.
                              Ref. CR13.F7 1970
An etymological dictionary of heraldic terms which includes Afrikaans heraldic terms. The encyclopedic coverage supplies information on the devising, granting, and usage of armorial bearings, banners, crests, supporters, and quarters as well as a brief account of all the authentic orders of chivalry. Civil and military state orders of merit and decoration are included.

———. *Shield and Crest: An Account of the Art and Science of Heraldry*. New York: Sterling Publishing Co., 1961.
                              Ref. CR21.F7 1961
Offers historical background on the development of the art and science of heraldry. There are descriptions of and explanations for most of the symbols and signs used in heraldry. Glossary and index of illustrations; general index.

Grant, Francis J., ed. *The Manual of Heraldry*. Edinburgh: John Grant, 1948.   Ref. CR23.G8 1948
A concise dictionary of heraldic terms including a chapter on the order of precedency.

Murtaugh, Paul. *Your Irish Coats-of-Arms*. New York: The Ainsworth Co., 1960.   Ref. CR1672.M8 1960
Colored plates of arms for over 2,000 Irish names. Comprehensive name index keyed to the plates.

Parker, James. *A Glossary of Terms Used in Heraldry*. Rutland, Vt.: Charles E. Tuttle, 1970.   Ref. CR1618.P3 1970

Arranged in one alphabetical list, this book defines and describes heraldic terms. There are 1,000 illustrations, including several color plates.

Rietstap, Johannes Baptiste. *Armorial Général.* Baltimore: Genealogical Publishing Co., 1965. Ref. CR1179.R52 1965
Standard work on European arms, containing more than 100,000 family names, arranged A–Z by family. Illustrations are not included, and the text is in French.

———. *General Illustrated Armorial.* Illus. and ed. V. & H. Rolland. 3d ed. Lyons: Société de Sauvegarde Historique, [1953?]. 6 vols. Ref. CR1179.R52 Suppl.
A supplement to *Armorial Général,* containing illustrations of all the coats of arms described therein.

Zieber, Eugene. *Heraldry in America.* Philadelphia: J. B. Lippincott for Bailey, Banks, and Biddle, 1895.
Ref. CR1202.Z6
Large section devoted to discussion and description of American state and organizational seals, ecclesiastical seals, colonial societies, and American orders.

Periodicals

Because the periodical literature in the area of genealogy and heraldry is extensive, the reader is urged to consult *Ulrich's International Periodicals Directory* (Z6941.U5, latest edition available in the Reference Room). Under the subject heading "Genealogy and Heraldry" are listed numerous specialized and regional genealogical publications that may be of interest to the researcher. Subscription information is provided.

The following works should also be consulted.

Sperry, Kip. *A Survey of American Genealogical Periodicals and Periodical Indexes.* Detroit: Gale Research Company, 1978.
Ref. Z5313.U5S65
Invaluable attempt to list and describe known genealogical periodical indexes. Select list of genealogical periodicals. Author, title, and subject indexes.

There are three indexes to genealogical periodicals that will acquaint the user with much of the specialized literature in the field.

Genealogical Periodical Annual Index. Bowie, Md.: George E. Russell, 1962–69. 8 vols.   Ref. CS42.G467

Jacobus, Donald Lines. *Index to Genealogical Periodicals.* Baltimore: Genealogical Publishing Co., 1963–64. 3 vols.
                                                      Ref. Z5313.U5J19

Sperry, Kip. *Index to Genealogical Periodical Literature, 1960–1977.* Detroit: Gale Research Company, 1979.
                                                      Ref. Z5313.U5S64

The following list of basic genealogical periodicals available in the Alderman Library has been compiled with special emphasis on publications related to Virginia genealogy. It should be noted that the library has issues of numerous other genealogical periodicals not included in this listing.

The basic guide for finding magazines in Alderman Library is a computer-produced list of periodical and newspaper titles that indicates call numbers and locations of all current issues. Copies of this list are found in the Reference Room, Periodicals Room, and the Main Hall. To determine the exact holdings and locations of back issues, consult the card catalog in the Main Hall.

Daughters of the American Revolution Magazine.
    Stacks. E202.5.A12. Incomplete holdings, 1892 to date.

The Magazine of Albemarle County History.
    Ref. F232.A3M3 (also in Stacks). Complete holdings.

National Genealogical Society Quarterly.
    Stacks. CS42.N4. Incomplete holdings, 1937–53. No current holdings.

Pennsylvania Magazine of History and Biography.
    Stacks. F146.P65. Complete holdings.

Sons of the American Revolution [*Magazine*].
    Stacks. E202.3.A5. Incomplete holdings, 1907 to date.

Tyler's Quarterly Historical and Genealogical Magazine.
Ref. F221.T95 (also in Stacks). Complete holdings, ceased publication 1952. Indexed in E. G. Swem's *Virginia Historical Index.*

Virginia Genealogical Society Bulletin.
Rare Book Coll. F225.V47. Complete holdings.

Virginia Genealogist.
Rare Book Coll. F225.V48. Complete holdings.

Virginia Magazine of History and Biography.
Ref. F221.V91 (also in Stacks). Complete holdings. Indexed in E. G. Swem's *Virginia Historical Index.*

William and Mary Quarterly.
Ref. F221.W71 (also in Rare Book Coll.). Complete holdings. Indexed in E. G. Swem's *Virginia Historical Index.*

II. FOREIGN SOURCES

Great Britain

Bibliographies and Indexes

Barrow, Geoffrey, B. *The Genealogist's Guide: An Index to Printed British Pedigrees and Family Histories, 1950–1975.* London: Research Publishing Co., 1977.

Ref. Z5313.G69B36 1977

Continues the coverage of Marshall's *Genealogist's Guide* and Whitmore's *Genealogical Guide* (below).

Crisp, Frederick Arthur. *List of Parish Registers and Other Genealogical Works.* London: F. A. Crisp, 1899; Cleveland: Microphoto, 1963.

Stacks. Z5313.G69C9 1963 and Film 2515

Falley, Margaret D. *Irish and Scotch-Irish Ancestral Research: A Guide to the Genealogical Records, Methods, and Sources in Ireland.* Evanston, Ill.: By the Author, 1962. 2 vols.

Rare Book Coll. CS483.F25 1961

Deals comprehensively with every phase of record searching in Ireland and Irish records in the United States. Includes discussion of genealogical materials destroyed in 1922.

Ferguson, Joan P. S. *Scottish Family Histories Held in Scottish Libraries.* Edinburgh: The Scottish Central Library, 1960.

Ref. CS478.F4 1960

A union list of Scottish family histories held in Scottish libraries excluding the National Library of Scotland. The arrangement is alphabetical by family name. Manuscript material is not included.

Filby, P. William. *American & British Genealogy and Heraldry: A Selected List of Books.* (See chapter III.)

Gardner, David E., and Frank Smith. *Genealogical Research in England and Wales.* Salt Lake City: Bookcraft, 1956–59. 2 vols.

Ref. CS414.G3 1956

Guide to record sources in England and Wales. Arrangement is by record type, with information concerning the history of the records, how to find them, and how to search them. Volume 2, chapter 9 contains an arrangement by county which lists county records and publications of help to the researcher. County maps are included. Volume 2 also contains five chapters on the use and interpretation of probate records.

Gibson, Jeremy. *Wills and Where to Find Them.* Chichester, Eng.: Phillimore and Company Limited, 1974.
> Stacks. CD1068.A2G5 1974

Locations of wills, by county, for England, Scotland, Ireland, Wales, the Channel Islands, and the Isle of Man. Index of courts. Supersedes *Wills and Their Whereabouts* (1963), by Anthony J. Camp.

Kaminkow, Marion J. *Genealogical Manuscripts in British Libraries: A Descriptive Guide.* Baltimore: Magna Charta, 1967.
> Ref. Z5305.G7K3 1967

Result of a mail survey of manuscripts in libraries in Great Britain and Ireland. The arrangement is by location with descriptions of holdings in each of the libraries surveyed. Indexes.

_____. *A New Bibliography of British Genealogy with Notes.* Baltimore: Magna Charta, 1965.   Ref. Z5313.G69K3 1965
A fine table of contents and complete index allow the user to survey British genealogical materials and sources. A lengthy section on British counties lists the key sources available for particular jurisdictions.

Marshall, George W. *The Genealogist's Guide.* Guilford, Eng.: Billing and Sons, 1903.   Ref. Z5313.G69M42 1903
The standard guide to printed British genealogies. It is arranged by family name and contains complete information on the location of the genealogies. Continued by Whitmore (below) and Barrow (above).

Stuart, Margaret. *Scottish Family History.* Edinburgh: Oliver and Boyd, 1930.   Ref. Z5313.S4S9 1930
A bibliography of printed material on Scottish families, including information found in *Burke's Peerage* and *The Scots*

Peerage. The arrangement is alphabetical by family name. This volume also contains a concise introductory essay on writing family histories.

Wagner, Anthony Richard. *English Genealogy*. 2d ed., enlarged. Oxford: Clarendon Press, 1972.   Ref. CS414.W3 1972
A general historical overview of English family lines. "About two-thirds of the book deal with the social and historical backgrounds and the subject matter of English genealogy. The rest is concerned with the study, literature, and technique of the subject and the nature of the record evidence on which they rest."

Whitmore, J. B. *A Genealogical Guide: An Index to British Pedigrees in Continuation of Marshall's Genealogical Guide*. London: Walford, 1953.   Ref. Z5313.G69W45 1953
Updates and expands the work of Marshall's *Genealogist's Guide* (see above) to include genealogical publications issued between 1903 and 1950. Continued by Barrow (above).

Biographical Dictionaries
The following is a brief list of dictionaries of British biography. Additional biographical information on British citizens can be found in the next section, Peerage, and in chapter I under Biographical Dictionaries.

Boase, Frederic. *Modern English Biography; Containing Many Thousand Concise Memoirs of Persons Who Have Died between the Years 1851–1900 with an Index of the Interesting Matter*. Reprint. London: Frank Cass, 1965. 6 vols.
Ref. CT773.B6 1965
A valuable source for biographical information on the lesser-known personalities of the nineteenth century. The work has a greater coverage of the national and local celebrities of the nineteenth century than the *Dictionary of National Biography* (below). The volumes contain approximately 30,000 entries. Sources of biographical information are noted, and there is an excellent analytical index in each volume.

Cambridge University. *Alumni Cantabrigienses: A Biographical List of All Known Students, Graduates, and Holders of Office at the University of Cambridge, from the Earliest Times to 1900.*

Comp. John Venn and J. A. Venn. Cambridge: The University Press, 1922–54. 6 vols.　　　　　Ref. LF124.A2 1900
Entries include date of matriculation and age at the time of matriculation, college entered, and degrees earned. Often parents' names and the names of relatives who attended Cambridge are included. The arrangement is alphabetical by surname.

Dictionary of National Biography. Ed. Leslie Stephen and Sidney Lee. Reprint. London: Oxford University Press, [1950]. 22 vols.　　　　　Ref. DA28.D4 1950

＿＿. 2d–8th Supplements. London: Oxford University Press, 1912–81.
The major scholarly biographical dictionary of noteworthy persons of the British Isles and the British colonies including prominent American colonists. The *DNB* is a historical dictionary which includes only deceased persons. The 8th Supplement brings the scope of the work from "the earliest historic times" through 1970. Each article is signed, and bibliographies and sources of information are provided. The arrangement is alphabetical.

Oxford University. *Alumni Oxonienses: The Members of the University of Oxford, 1500–1886; Their Parentage, Birthplace, and Year of Birth, with a Record of Their Degrees. . . .* Revised and annotated by Joseph Foster. Reprint. Nendeln: Kraus Reprint, 1968. 4 vols.　　　　　Ref. LF524.A22 1968
An alphabetical listing of the alumni of the University of Oxford giving, in most cases, parents' names, date and place of birth, and degrees granted by the University.

Peerage

For the genealogist who has been successful in tracing his ancestry beyond the settler who came from Europe and is attempting to discover a relation to notable families, the following handbooks should be helpful. This list is limited to the English, Scottish, and Irish peerage, knightage, baronetage, and landed gentry, and is only a small sampling of the library's holdings. There have been numerous editions of Burke and Debrett; many of the earlier editions can be found in the Rare Books Department. Patrons are urged to consult the subject catalog for additional information.

The most direct entries in the subject catalog are "Name of country—Peerage" or "Name of country—Nobility"(e.g., "Germany—Peerage" or "Germany—Nobility").

Angerville, Count d', ed. *Living Descendants of Blood Royal in America*. London: World Nobility and Peerage, 1963. 2 vols. Ref. CS55.A29 1959
Contains pedigrees of those contemporary Americans whose ancestry can be traced to the kings of England, Scotland, and France. Page xxvii provides a list of seventeenth-century immigrants of royal blood who came to America from Europe. Index.

Burke, Sir John Bernard. *Burke's Family Index*. London: Burke's Peerage; New York: Arco, 1976. Ref. CS420.B84
Indexes various publications by Burke (e.g., *Peerage and Baronetage, Landed Gentry,* etc.), giving "The most complete and up-to-date version of a family's narrative pedigree in a Burke's publication since 1826." "Bibliography of Burke's, 1826–1976" is a useful inclusion.

_____. *Burke's Genealogical and Heraldic History of the Peerage, Baronetage, and Knightage*. Ed. Peter Townend. 105th ed. London: Burke's Peerage, 1970.
Ref. CS420.B85 105th ed. 1970
Latest edition in the Reference Room; earlier editions in stacks. This is the only one of the currently published peerages that includes complete lineage. Peerage and baronetage are arranged alphabetically by title; archbishops, bishops, knightage, and Privy Council members are included; there are articles on royal lineage and tables of precedence, orders, decorations, and medals.

_____. *Genealogical and Heraldic History of the Landed Gentry, Founded 1836 by John Burke and Sir Bernard Burke*. Ed. Peter Townend. 18th ed. London: Burke's Peerage, 1965–72. 3 vols. Ref. CS425.B8 1965
Biographical sketch of present head of family, names of wife and children, lineage, arms, and seat. Includes England, Scotland, and Wales.

_____. *Genealogical and Heraldic History of the Landed Gentry Including American Families with British Ancestry.* London: Burke's Peerage, 1939.   Ref. CS425.B8 1939
This is the only edition that includes American families with British ancestry (pp. 2539–3021).

_____. *A Genealogical and Heraldic History of the Landed Gentry of Great Britain and Ireland.* 5th ed. London: Harrison, 1871.   Ref. CS425.B8 1871
This edition includes the Irish gentry.

_____. *Genealogical and Heraldic History of the Landed Gentry of Ireland.* Ed. L. G. Pine. 4th ed. London: Burke's Peerage, 1958.   Ref. CS490.B8 1958
Devoted entirely to lineage of the Irish landed gentry.

_____. *A Genealogical History of the Dormant, Abeyant, Forfeited, and Extinct Peerages of the British Empire.* New ed. London: Harrison, 1883; London: W. Clowes, 1962.
                    Ref. CS422.B88 1883 1962 ed.
                    (1866 ed. is in Rare Book Coll.)
Useful for descendants and ancestors of peers.

[Cokayne, G. E.] *The Complete Peerage of England, Scotland, Ireland, Great Britain, and the United Kingdom.* New ed. Ed. Vicary Gibbs. London: The St. Catherine Press, 1910–40. 13 vols.   Ref. CS421.C55 1910
The most complete historical record of the British peerage, giving full biographical data and pedigree. The volumes are well documented and include bibliographical references to sources of information. Volume 13 covers peerage creations from 1901 to 1938. The arrangement of all volumes is alphabetical by peerage. There is no comprehensive index to the *Complete Peerage.*

Debrett's Peerage and Baronetage; with Her Majesty's Royal Warrant Holders. Ed. P. W. Montague-Smith. London: Debrett's Peerage Limited, 1980.   Ref. CS420.D32
Does not supply complete lineage; however, coverage of female collaterals is much more extensive than Burke's *Peerage.*

Koller, F., ed. *International Register of Nobility*. Brussels: Les Editions Biographiques, 1959–60.   Ref. CS404.I5
Genealogical dictionary of contemporary European nobility, including eastern European countries that are now Communist. The arrangement is alphabetical. Index.

MacLysaght, Edward. *Irish Families: Their Names, Arms, and Origins*. Dublin: Hodges Figgis, 1957.
                    Ref. CS498.M3 1957

———. *More Irish Families*. Galway and Dublin: O'Gorman, 1960.   Ref. CS498.M32 1960

Paul, Sir James Balfour, ed. *The Scots Peerage, Founded on Wood's Edition of Sir Robert Douglas's* Peerage of Scotland; Containing an Historical and Genealogical Account of the Nobility of That Kingdom. Edinburgh: David Douglas, 1904–14. 9 vols.   Ref. CS468.P3 1904
Narrative biographies of titleholders and all issue in the male line. Volume 9 contains a comprehensive name index.

Sanders, I. J. *English Baronies: A Study of Their Origin and Descent*. Oxford: Clarendon Press, 1960.   Ref. CS429.S3 1960
Histories of more than 200 estates, concentrating upon the descent of the barony. There is a comprehensive index.

Walford, Edward. *The County Families of the United Kingdom, or Royal Manual of the Titled and Untitled Aristocracy of Great Britain and Ireland*. 6th ed. London: Robert Hardwicke, 1871.   Ref. CS419.W3 1871
Descent, births, marriages, education and appointments, heirs apparent or presumptive, and offices and residences are all included in this work. It may be viewed as a "dictionary of the upper ten thousand" in British society in the latter half of the nineteenth century. The arrangement is alphabetical.

Other Foreign Countries

Once a family line has been traced back to another country, little research can be done without visiting that country to examine its records or finding an appropriate collection of secondary source materials in the United States. Alderman Library has a few guides and bibliographies relating to foreign genealogy as well as a few printed genealogies. To find these, consult the subject card catatlog under the name of the country in question (e.g., "France—Genealogy").

Following is a brief list of the more outstanding guides and bibliographies dealing with foreign genealogy, with emphasis on noble family lines.

Burke's Royal Families of the World. Vol. 1: *Europe and Latin America;* Vol. 2: *Africa and the Middle East.* London: Burke's Peerage, 1977–81.   Ref. CS27.B9
Like Stokvis (below) in limiting its coverage to royalty but not as detailed as that work.

Henning, Eckart, and Wolfgang Ribbe. *Handbuch der Genealogie.* Neustadt an der Aisch: Degener, 1972.
Stacks. CS11.H35
A comprehensive guide to genealogical and heraldic research in Germanic countries. Includes an extensive bibliography and an index. Good source to consult before visiting Germany for research.

Kneschke, Ernst Heinrich. *Neues allgemeines deutsches Adels-Lexikon.* Leipzig: Friedrich Voigt, 1859–70; Hildesheim: Georg Olms, 1973. 9 vols.   Ref. CS617.K6 1973
A dictionary of German noble family lines. Entries are generally brief but may give extensive family history, mentioning more important family members by name. Armorial shields are described in many cases.

La Chenaye-Desbois, François Alexandre Aubert de. *Dictionnaire de la noblesse, contenant les généalogies, l'historie, & la chronologie des familles nobles de la France.* . . . 3d ed. Paris, 1863–76; Nendeln: Kraus Reprint, 1969. 19 vols.
Ref. CS587.L2 1969
Contains genealogies of the nobility of France and French territories, with outlines of other European royal houses.

Municio Cristobal, Benito, and Luis García Cubero. *Bibliografía heráldico-genealógico-nobiliaria de la Biblioteca Nacional de Madrid.* Madrid: Hidalguía, 1958. 2 vols.
Stacks. Z5319.M8

Bibliography of holdings of the Biblioteca Nacional de Madrid in genealogy and heraldry, arranged by author. Index at end of vol. 2.

Saffroy, Gaston. *Bibliographie généalogique, héraldique, et nobiliaire de la France.* . . . Paris: Gaston Saffroy, 1968–79. 4 vols.
Ref. Z5305.F7S22
An extensive bibliography of French genealogy, heraldry, and nobility, including books, articles, manuscripts, and maps. Each entry includes the Bibliothèque Nationale number of the work or, if the item is not in the Bibliothèque Nationale, the location of the work at another library. Vol. 1: general works. Vol. 2: provinces, colonies, immigrants, and emigrants. Vol. 3: families. Vol. 4 is an index to the set.

Stokvis, A. M. H. J. *Manuel d'histoire, de généaologie, et de chronologie de tous les états du globe, depuis les temps les plus reculés jusqu'à nos jours.* Leiden: Brill, 1888–93; Amsterdam: B. M. Israël, 1966. 4 vols.
Ref. D11.S87 1966
Outlines the genealogies of major dynasties and royal houses of all countries in the world.

III. UNITED STATES SOURCES

Bibliographies and Indexes

Included below are bibliographies and indexes of American family histories. Several of the works in this list contain exhaustive genealogies of important American families and include collateral as well as lineal descent.

American Genealogist; Being a Catalogue of Family Histories. 5th ed. Albany: Joel Munsell's Sons, 1900.

Ref. Z5313.U5W61 1900

A list of the title pages of books and pamphlets on genealogies published in America from 1771 to 1900. The arrangement is alphabetical by family name.

Armstrong, Zella. *Notable Southern Families.* Chattanooga: The Lookout Publishing Co., 1918–34. 7 vols.

Stacks. CS61.A6

Complete genealogies of selected southern families, most of them original settlers of Tennessee.

Boddie, John Bennett. *Historical Southern Families.* Redwood City, Calif.: Pacific Coast Publishers, 1957–72. 17 vols. Rare Book Coll. CS69.B64 1957. Library has vols. 1–10, 12–17.

Burke's Presidential Families of the United States. Ed. Hugh Montgomery-Massingberd. 2d ed. London: Burke's Peerage Limited, 1981.   Ref. CS69.B82 1981
Includes native pedigree of each president, his lineage and descendants, and some collateral lines. There is a biography of each president, up to and including Ronald Reagan. Appendixes include a genealogy of Jefferson Davis, sketches of the vice-presidents, and tables showing royal descent of presidents.

Catalogue of American Genealogies in the Library of the Long Island Historical Society. New York: Long Island Historical Society, 1935.   Ref. Z5313.U5L8 1935
An alphabetical listing of individual and family genealogies in the Long Island Historical Society Library, whose collec-

tion totals over 8,200 items. It is particularly helpful to the genealogist searching for New England and New York families, although not strictly limited to this geographic area.

Filby, P. William. *American and British Genealogy and Heraldry: A Selected List of Books.* 2d ed. Chicago: American Library Association, 1975.   Ref. Z5311.F55 1975
A good bibliography of major books on genealogy and heraldry. For the United States there is a state-by-state arrangement of sources. Particularly helpful for locating secondary sources. Index.

Genealogical and Local History Books in Print. Comp. Netti Schreiner-Yantis. Springfield, Va., 1975–81. 3 vols.
                Ref. Z5313.U564
Lists family histories and family newsletters available for purchase. Surname indexes. Listings of publisher or vendor addresses.

Henry, Reginald Buchanan. *Genealogies of the Families of the Presidents.* Rutland, Vt.: Tuttle, 1935.   Stacks. CS69.H4
"The principal object of this work [is] . . . to bring together . . . many genealogies and fragments of genealogies of the families of the Presidents." The arrangement is chronological by president, and there is a comprehensive name index. Bibliography.

Index to American Genealogies. 5th rev. ed. New York: Joel Munsell, 1900.   Ref. Z5313.U5D94 1900
Lists titles of works that contain references to or genealogies of American families. The arrangement of the titles is alphabetical by family name.

Rider, Fremont, ed. *The American Genealogical-Biographical Index to American Genealogical, Biographical, and Local History Materials.* Middletown, Godfrey Memorial Library, 1952– .
(In progress.)   Ref. Z5313.U5A55 1952
This is one of the most important beginning sources. A surname index to numerous printed and published genealogies, the genealogical column of the *Boston Transcript* newspaper, the first census of the United States, and the 63

volumes of the Revolutionary War Records. Birth dates, when available, are recorded, as well as state location of the name indexed. The user should pay close attention to the list of sources from which the genealogies are drawn, since the list does not appear in every volume. Please note the explanation card on shelf beside the volumes in the Reference Room.

———. *American Genealogical Index*. Middletown, Conn.: Cooperating subscribing libraries, 1942–52. 48 vols.
Ref. CS44.A6 1942
Being replaced by *American Genealogical-Biographical Index* . . . (above).

Virkus, Frederick A., ed. *The Abridged Compendium of American Genealogy: First Families of America, a Genealogical Encyclopedia of the United States*. Chicago: A. N. Marquis, 1925. 6 vols.
Ref. CS69.V814 1925
Contains more than 7,000 lineages, primarily American families of colonial or Revolutionary ancestry. There is an alphabetical index at the end of each volume.

Zorn, Walter Lewis. *The Descendants of the Presidents of the United States of America*. 2d rev. ed. Monroe, Mich.: By the Author, 1955.
Stacks. CS69.Z5 1955
Lineal descendants of the presidents.

Biographical Dictionaries

The following brief list of American biographical dictionaries includes the most comprehensive standard works. Generally their coverage is limited to citizens and immigrants now deceased; foreign persons who have had an influential role in American history (for example, General Lafayette) are sometimes listed. For more general biographical dictionaries, consult chapter I of this guide. Foreign biographical dictionaries are listed in chapter II.

American Biography: A New Encyclopedia. New York: American Historical Society, 1916– . Vols. 1–13, 15, 35, 53, 58.
Ref. E176.A47
Includes many minor political figures of the nineteenth cen-

tury. The arrangement within the volumes is not alphabetical; it is therefore necessary to consult the index at the end of each volume. Coverage begins with the year 1865.

Appleton's Cyclopedia of American Biography. Ed. James G. Wilson and John Fiske. New York: D. Appleton, 1887. 6 vols.
Ref. E176.A659 1887
Contains over 15,000 "prominent native and adopted citizens of the United States . . . from the earliest settlement of the country. . . . The great aim has been to include all noteworthy persons of the New World." The arrangement is alphabetical, and the volumes contain numerous plates.

Dictionary of American Biography. New York: Scribners, 1928–37. 20 vols. and index. Ref. E176.D56 1928

_____. Supplements 1–6. New York: Scribner, 1944–80.
Provides coverage through 1960 and includes an index to all supplements. The chief American scholarly biographical dictionary, the *DAB* includes noteworthy persons of all periods who lived in the territories that now comprise the United States. Each article includes a bibliography. The arrangement is alphabetical.

National Cyclopedia of American Biography. New York: J. T. White, 1892– . Vols. 1–73. (In progress.)
Ref. E176.N28 1892
A very comprehensive American biographical dictionary. The standards for inclusion in the *National Cyclopedia* are less restrictive than those of the *DAB*. Because the arrangement is not alphabetical, it is necessary to consult the indexes.

History, Records, and Genealogies

Colonial

The genealogical researcher who is attempting to trace an emigrant ancestry must first determine the emigrant's identity and the port and date of landing. The following list of general sources includes several ship passenger lists and two major bibliographies of ship passenger lists (see Filby and Lancour below).

Banks, Charles Edward. *Topographical Dictionary of 2885 English Emigrants to New England, 1620–1650*. Philadelphia: E. E. Brownell, 1937. Ref. F3.B35
Alphabetical arrangement of English counties, listing the name of the emigrant, his parish, ship's name, the New England town he settled in, and the reference source of the information. Also included are indexes of wives and children of emigrants, parishes, English counties and shires, ships carrying emigrants, and New England towns.

Colonial Dames of America. *Ancestral Records and Portraits: A Compilation from the Archives of Chapter I of the Colonial Dames of America*. New York: The Grafton Press, 1910. 2 vols. Rare Book Coll. E186.5.B25 1910
Contains the lineages of descendants of the original colonists from the *Mayflower*, the Huguenots, and the settlers of the southern colonies who are members of the Colonial Dames of America. Index.

Filby, P. William, ed. *Passenger and Immigration Lists Bibliography, 1538–1900; Being a Guide to Published Lists of Arrivals in the United States and Canada*. Detroit: Gale Research, 1981. Ref. Z7164
A revision and expansion of Lancour (below). Coverage is extended to 1900. Lists about five times the number of lists described by 1963 edition of Lancour. Subject index. No index of authors and contributors, or of ship names, as in Lancour.

Hardy, Stella Pickett. *Colonial Families of the Southern States of America*. New York: Tobias A. Wright, 1911. Rare Book Coll. CS61.H3 1911
Indexes over 10,000 names, ports of entry and departure, and coats of arms. Genealogies of selected colonial families. Alphabetical arrangement by surname; index of all names.

Holmes, Frank R. *Directory of the Ancestral Heads of New England Families, 1620–1700*. Baltimore: Genealogical Publishing Co., 1964. Ref. CS61.H6 1964
Historical and biographical information on New England

family heads and members of these families. Arrangement by family name.

Hotten, John Camden, ed. *The Original Lists of Persons of Quality, Emigrants, Religious Exiles, Political Rebels, Serving Men Sold for a Term of Years, Apprentices, Children Stolen, Maidens Pressed, and Others Who Went from Great Britain to the American Plantation, 1600–1700.* New York: G. A. Baker & Co., 1931.   Ref. E187.5.H795 1931
Taken from the papers of the Public Record Office, England, this work includes, when available, the ages of emigrants, their former English homes, the names of the ships that carried them, and other pertinent information. There is a muster roll of the inhabitants of Virginia and a list of the living and dead in Virginia in 1623. Comprehensive index.

Lancour, Harold. *A Bibliography of Ship Passenger Lists, 1538–1825.* 3d ed., revised and enlarged by Richard J. Wolfe. New York: New York Public Library, 1963.
                                Ref. Z7164.I3L2 1963
Emigrant lists of persons who came to America before 1826. Annotated bibliography by state of port of entry. Appendix I contains lists of ship passengers and emigrants arriving after 1825; Appendix II describes the passenger arrival records in the National Archives. There is also an index of ship names. An excellent source for information on emigrants to America from all parts of Europe.

MacKenzie, George Norbury. *Colonial Families of the United States of America.* New York and Boston: The Grafton Press, 1907–20. 7 vols.   Ref. CS61.M2
History, genealogy, and armorial bearings of colonial families who lived in the American colonies from the settlement of Jamestown (1607) to the Revolution (1775). There is an index.

Passenger and Immigration Lists Index: A Guide to Published Arrival Records of About 500,000 Passengers Who Came to the United States and Canada in the 17th, 18th, and 19th Centuries. Ed. P. William Filby, with Mary K. Meyer. Detroit: Gale Research, 1981. 3 vols.   Ref. CS68.P36 1981

Indexes, in one alphabet, names from over 300 published sources. Information about each passenger edited to a standard format: (1) name; (2) age; (3) place of arrival; (4) year of arrival; (5) source book; (6) page number of source; (7) list of all accompanying passengers, noting age and their relationship to the main passenger. Accompanying passengers are cross-referenced. The publisher plans to issue periodic supplements.

Sherwood, George Frederic Tudor. *American Colonists in English Records*. London: J. Sherwood, 1932. 2 vols.
Ref. E187.5.S52 1932
Arranged by year, this work lists the direct references in English record sources to American colonists as well as some passenger lists not included in Hotten (above).

Revolutionary War
Genealogists concerned with documenting the Revolutionary War service of an individual should begin by consulting the sources listed here. For information on Virginians who served in the Revolutionary War, see chapter IV. For states other than Virginia, the patron should consult the subject catalog under the following entry: "Name of State [e.g., Massachusetts]—History—Revolution—Registers, lists, etc."

Daughters of the American Revolution. *DAR Patriot Index*. Washington, D.C.: National Society of the Daughters of the American Revolution, 1966.   Ref. E202.5.A152 1966
Contains the names of Revolutionary patriots who served between 1774 and 1783 and whose identity has been established by the DAR. The index lists over 105,000 names. Arranged alphabetically by surname; entries include birth and death dates, name of spouse, and type and place of military service. Over 4,500 names added in supplements.

_____. *Lineage Book*. Harrisonburg, Va., and Washington, D.C.: National Society of the Daughters of the American Revolution, 1890–1905. 54 vols.   Stacks. E202.5.A15
According to the charter of the DAR the "sole requisite for eligibility to membership . . . is proven lineal descent from an ancestor who . . . rendered material aid to the cause of In-

dependence as a patriot, as soldier or sailor, or as a civil officer in one of the several colonies." These volumes contain the lineages of the charter members of the DAR. Volumes are indexed both by DAR member and by patriot name.

Daughters of the American Revolution Magazine. *Genealogical Guide: Master Index of Genealogy in the Daughters of the American Revolution Magazine, Volumes 1–84, 1892–1950.* Washington, D.C.: DAR Magazine, 1951.
Ref. E202.5.A12 Master Index Vols. 1–84
Indexes the *Daughters of the American Revolution Magazine.* Copies of the magazine are available in the stacks under E202.5.A12.

Heitman, Francis B. *Historical Register of Officers of the Continental Army during the War of the Revolution.* New, rev., enlarged ed. Washington, D.C.: Rare Book Shop Publishing Co., 1914.   Ref. E255.H47 1914
Brief descriptions of army careers of each Continental Army officer. Includes a list of the generals and field officers of the Continental Line with their dates of service and the artillery or infantry regiments they commanded.

Saffell, William. *Records of the Revolutionary War . . . .* New York: Pudney and Russell, 1858.
Rare Book Coll. E203.S13 1858
Contains names of officers and enlisted men of regiments, companies, and corps, with the dates of their commissions and enlistments. There is also a list of the officers of the Continental Army who acquired the right to lands, commutation, and/or half pay, as well as the Revolutionary pension lists. Saffell includes some correspondence of Revolutionary War officers, a brief history on the Society of the Cincinnati with a list of the original members, and (on pp. 489–510) the acts of the Virginia legislature concerning bounty lands. The index is in the front of the volume on page 14; there is an extensive table of contents.

Civil War

The major repository of Civil War documents is the National Archives in Washington, D.C. The following brief list of general sources will provide a helpful starting point, particularly the two guides that describe Confederate and Federal Civil War documents in the National Archives. For further information on Virginians in the Civil War, consult chapter IV. The patron is also urged to consult the *Subject Headings Used in the Dictionary Catalog of the Library of Congress* (Z695.U47 1980) (available in the Reference Room and the Main Hall) for subject entries related to the Civil War. For example, regimental histories are entered in the subject catalog under the name of the regiment.

Beers, Henry Putney. *Guide to the Archives of the Government of the Confederate States of America.* Washington, D. C.: National Archives, 1968.   Pub. Docs. GS4.6²:C76
Contains general descriptions of the records of agencies of the Confederate government, including the Congress and the judicial and executive branches. Of particular importance and interest to the genealogist are the chapters devoted to the War Department and the Navy Department of the Confederacy. Both chapters include lengthy sections on regiments, battalions, companies, and commanders and refer the reader to the correct record group in the National Archives. There is a comprehensive index.

Confederate States of America. Army. Department of Northern Virginia. *The Appomattox Roster: A List of the Paroles of the Army of Northern Virginia, Issued at Appomattox Court House on April 9, 1865.* New York: Antiquarian Press, 1962.
                                        Ref. E548.C66 1962
Lists of Confederate officers, noncommissioned officers, and enlisted men who surrendered with the Army of Northern Virginia and were paroled. There is a comprehensive surname index. The work is helpful in determining battalions, regiments, and companies in which Confederate soldiers served.

Mundan, Kenneth W., and Henry Putney Beers. *Guide to the Federal Archives Relating to the Civil War.* Washington, D.C.: The National Archives, 1962.   Ref. CD3047.M8 1962
The companion volume to the *Guide to the Archives . . . of the Confederate States of America* (above), this volume is also arranged by agency name. "Records of a general character are described, and there follow separate descriptions of the records of component bureaus or other offices, each usually pre-

ceded by a historical statement." The chapters on the War Department, the Department of the Navy, and the Department of the Interior Pension Office are most useful. Well indexed.

Warner, Ezra J. *Generals in Blue: Lives of the Union Commanders*. [Baton Rouge]: Louisiana State University Press, 1964.

Ref. E467.W29

Biographical sketches of Union generals. Includes several useful appendixes, bibliographic notes on each entry, and a complete bibliography of sources. The arrangement is alphabetical.

———. *Generals in Gray: Lives of the Confederate Commanders*. [Baton Rouge]: Louisiana State University Press, 1959.

Ref. E467.W3 1959

Concise biographical sketches of Confederate generals. Format identical to *Generals in Blue*, above.

Individual States

For genealogical works on individual states other than Virginia, for which an extensive bibliography follows, check the subject card catalog under the name of the state or county (e.g., "Georgia—Genealogy"; "Macon County, Georgia—Genealogy"). Some of the general genealogy guides in chapter I, such as the American Society of Genealogists' *Genealogical Research Methods and Sources*, also list important sources for research on other states.

The following works may be useful for locating historical information on a particular locality.

Directory of Historical Societies and Agencies in the United States and Canada. Nashville: American Association for State and Local History, 1971– .   Ref. E151.A508 (current ed. only)
A listing by state and city of local historical societies. The information in this directory includes name, address, titles of publications, and "major programs" such as museum, archives, library, oral history, markers, and manuscripts. Index by name of society.

Peterson, Clarence Stewart. *Bibliography of Local Histories*. Baltimore, 1966–67. 2 vols.   Ref. Z1250.P465
Vol. 1: Atlantic States. Vol. 2: Thirty-five States beyond the

Atlantic States. A bibliography of local histories, other than county histories, arranged by state.

_____. *Consolidated Bibliography of County Histories in Fifty States in 1961.* 2d ed. Baltimore: Genealogical Publishing Co., 1963.   Ref. Z1250.P47 1963
A bibliography of county histories arranged by state and county.

IV. VIRGINIA SOURCES

Bibliographies and Indexes

The following works are major reference sources for genealogical and historical works on Virginia. For beginning research, the three basic works are Brown, Stewart, and Swem.

Brown, Stuart E. *Virginia Genealogies: A Trial List of Printed Books and Pamphlets.* Berryville, Va.: Virginia Book Company, 1967–80. 2 vols.   Ref. Z5313.U6V76
  Printed catalog cards of printed Virginia genealogies held by the Library of Congress, Virginia State Library, University of Virginia, and the Virginia Historical Society. Has an index by family name, with items referred to by page and item number.

Marcell, Susan O. "Virginia History and Biography: A Guide to Materials in Alderman Library, Including a Bibliography of County Histories."   Inquire at Reference Desk.
  This is a loose-leaf listing, by county, of local history sources. It is revised and annotated periodically.

Passano, Eleanor Phillips. *An Index of Source Records of Maryland: Genealogical, Biographical, Historical.* Baltimore: Genealogical Publishing Company, 1967.   Ref. Z1293.P3 1967
  Primarily an index of family names with a listing of institutions that hold papers or genealogies relating to these families. The full names and addresses of the institutions included can be found on page v of the introduction. The book also includes a comprehensive bibliography, a listing of church records, census lists, ship passenger lists, and tombstone inscriptions. Although primarily a Maryland source, this can be very helpful in Virginia research.

Stewart, Robert A. *Index to Printed Virginia Genealogies.* Richmond: Old Dominion Press, 1930.
                    Ref. Z5313.U6V8 1930
  A basic index to Virginia genealogies, together with Brown above. The "Key and Bibliography," pp. 5–36, indexes by

family name a large selection of printed historical and genealogical sources. The call numbers of all sources held by
Alderman Library as of 1975 have been added to the key of
the Reference Room copy.

Swem, Earl Gregg. *Virginia Historical Index.* Reprint. Gloucester,
Mass., Peter Smith Press, 1965. 4 vols.
        Ref. F221.S93 1965 (also in Rare Book Coll.)
Comprehensive subject index through 1930 of the follow-
ing: *Calendar of Virginia State Papers, Hening's Statutes,
Lower Norfolk County Virginia Antiquary, Virginia Historical
Register, Tyler's Quarterly, Virginia Magazine of History and
Biography,* and the *William and Mary Quarterly,* 1st and 2d
series. An essential source for the Virginia genealogist. Kept
in Reference on index table 5 near the materials indexed.

Virginia Books and Pamphlets Presently Available. Berryville, Va.:
Virginia Book Company, 1972.   Ref. Z1345.V76
An attempt to list the names of authors, titles, prices, and
publishers of all currently available books and pamphlets on
Virginia. Part 1: unofficial publications and publications of
the U.S. government and its agencies; indexed. Part 2: publications of the Commonwealth of Virginia and its agencies;
not indexed.

Virginia Local History. Richmond: Virginia State Library, 1971.
        Ref. Z1345.V91 1971
A bibliography of county, city, and town histories, arranged
alphabetically by place name.

Virginia. State Library. *Lists of the Court Records of the Virginia
Counties and Cities on Microfilm in the Archives Division.* Richmond, 1969. 2 vols.   Ref. F232.A12V5
Alphabetically listed, by county, with independent cities at
end.

Biographical Dictionaries

Brock, Robert Alonzo. *Virginia and Virginians.* Richmond: H. H.
Hardesty, 1888–89. 2 vols.   Ref. F225.B7 1888

Includes a general history of Virginia. Table of contents; no index.

Bruce, Philip Alexander. *Virginia: Rebirth of the Old Dominion.* Chicago: Lewis Publishing Co., 1929. 5 vols.
Stacks. F226.B88 1929
Volumes 3–5 contain biographies of living Virginians, stressing family histories. Use as a companion to *History of Virginia* and Tyler's *Encyclopedia of Virginia Biography* (below).

History of Virginia. Chicago: American Historical Society, 1929. 6 vols.
Ref. F226.H67
Volumes 4–6: Virginia Biography. Gives much information on family backgrounds of mostly late nineteenth- and early twentieth-century Virginians. Indexed at front of volume 1.

Johnston, Frederick. *Memorials of Old Virginia Clerks.* Lynchburg, Va.: J. P. Bell, 1888.
Ref. F225.J73
Arranged by county, lists clerks' names and dates of service, 1634–1888; includes about 100 biographical sketches. Indexed.

Men of Mark in Virginia. Ed. Lyon Gardener Tyler. Washington, D.C.: Men of Mark Publishing Company, 1906–9. 5 vols.
Ref. F225.M53
A who's who of Virginia at the time of publication; gives detailed biographical sketches and many photographs. Index in each volume, with general index in volume 5.

Tyler, Lyon Gardener. *Encyclopedia of Virginia Biography.* New York: Lewis Historical Publishing Company, 1915. 5 vols.
Ref. F225.T97
Biographies of prominent Virginians, some with genealogical information. Volumes 1–3 follow historical sequence from the founding through the nineteenth century. Each volume has an index. Volumes 4–5 are the supplements, indexed in volume 5. Includes many photographs.

Virginia Lives: The Old Dominion Who's Who. Ed. Richard Lee Morton. Hopkinsville, Ky.: Historical Record Association, 1964.
Stacks. F225.V54 1964

A selective biographical list of "contemporary leaders" of Virginia who were living at the time of publication. Includes some photographs.

History

The following sources may prove useful to those researching Virginia genealogy. For a more extensive listing, consult the subject card catalog under "Virginia—History."

Barton, R. T. *Virginia Colonial Decisions.* Boston: The Boston Book Company, 1909. 2 vols.
Rare Book Coll. F229.V78 1909
Decided cases of the chief court of Virginia, 1729–43. The introduction has extensive descriptions of the government, the development of cities, the church, and the law and courts of the time. Good background material for research in this period. Index of names.

Bean, Robert Bennett. *The Peopling of Virginia.* Boston: Chapman & Grimes, 1938.   Stacks. F229.B43
A demographic study of the colonial period, and who settled where in Virginia. Describes county organization. Many names of early families and settlers are mentioned. Index.

Boogher, William Fletcher. *Gleanings of Virginia History.* Washington, D.C.: W. F. Boogher, 1903.   Stacks. F221.B72
A miscellany of Virginia records, historical notes, and a few Virginia genealogies.

Cocke, Charles Francis. *Parish Lines: Diocese of Southern Virginia.* Richmond: Virginia State Library, 1964.
Ref. BX5918.S59C6

———. *Parish Lines: Diocese of Southwestern Virginia.* Richmond: Virginia State Library, 1960.   Ref. BX5918.S922C6

———. *Parish Lines: Diocese of Virginia.* Richmond: Virginia State Library, 1967.   Ref. BX5918.V8C6
The above three works give a historical review of Virginia Episcopal parishes from colonial times to the present. Help-

ful in tracking down parish records by clarifying parish structure. Maps; index.

Goodwin, Edward Lewis. *The Colonial Church in Virginia* . . . . Milwaukee: Morehouse Publishing Company, 1927.
Ref. BX5917.V8G6 1927
Chiefly a history with biographical sketches of clergy. Part 2 includes "List of the Colonial Clergy in Virginia" and "Table of Counties, Parishes, and Ministers."

A Hornbook of Virginia History. Richmond: Virginia State Library, 1965. Ref. F226.V88 1965
Summarizes basic information about Virginia and its history. Includes a bibliography of Virginia historical sources. Most helpful to genealogists for its explanation of the counties, listing extinct counties and historical evolution of existing ones.

Howe, Henry. *Historical Collections of Virginia: Containing a Collection of the Most Interesting Facts, Traditions, Biographical Sketches, Anecdotes, &c. Relating to Its History and Antiquities.* Charleston, S.C.: Babcock & Company, 1845.
Ref. F226.H84 1845
Contains general historical information on Virginia, with a description and history of each county. Mentions prominent people. Brief index.

Kegley, Frederick Bittle. *Kegley's Virginia Frontier: The Beginning of the Southwest; The Roanoke of Colonial Days, 1740–1783.* Roanoke, Va.: The Southwest Virginia Historical Society, 1938. Ref. F229.K26 1938 (also in Stacks)
An important history of the area. The work contains numerous references to wills, deeds, marriages, surveys, and grants. Comprehensive index.

Manahan, John Eacott. "The Cavalier Remounted: A Study of the Origins of Virginia's Population." Ph.D. diss., University of Virginia, 1946.
Ref. U.Va. Dissertation 505 (also in Stacks)
A study of English immigrants. Appendix IV: "List of Voyages to Virginia with Many Passengers Listed, 1607–1700."

Meade, William. *Old Churches, Ministers, and Families of Virginia.*
Philadelphia: J. B. Lippincott Company, [1910?]. 2 vols.
Ref. F225.M485 1910a (also in Rare Book Coll. and Stacks)
A Virginia family history, first published in 1857, based on
family, church, and court records. Bound in at end of volume
2: Jennings Cropper Wise, *Wise's Digested Index and Genea-
logical Guide to Bishop Meade's* Old Churches, Ministers, and
Families of Virginia (Richmond, 1910).

Morton, Richard Lee. *Colonial Virginia.* Chapel Hill, N.C.: Uni-
versity of North Carolina Press, 1960. 2 vols.
Ref. F229.M7 1960 (also in Stacks, Mss., and Rare Book
Coll.)
A comprehensive history of colonial Virginia. Includes maps
and bibliographies. Index in volume 2.

Southwest Virginia and the Valley. Roanoke, Va.: A. D. Smith &
Company, 1892.   Stacks. F226.S75 1892
Historical sketches of the various counties and cities of the
area; biographical sketches of citizens prominent at the time
of publication. Index.

Summers, Lewis Preston. *Annals of Southwest Virginia, 1769–
1800.* Abingdon, Va.: L. P. Summers, 1929.
                Rare Book Coll. F226.S82 1929 (also in Stacks)
Includes deeds, wills, marriage records, land records, etc., of
Botetourt, Fincastle, Montgomery, Washington, and Wythe
counties. Revolutionary soldier list. Personal name index.

———. *History of Southwest Virginia, 1746–1786; Washington County,
1777–1870.* Richmond: J. L. Hill Printing Company, 1903.
                Stacks. F232.W3S92 1903 (also in Rare Book Coll.)
Contains abstracts from some Botetourt and Washington
County records.

Virginia. *Calendar of Virginia State Papers and Other Manuscripts.*
Richmond, 1875–93.   Ref. F221.V5 1875
Primary source material for early Virginia history. Includes
land patents and other documents. Indexed in Swem's *Virginia Historical Index.*

Virginia. Laws, statutes, etc. *The Laws of Virginia; Being a Supplement to Hening's* The Statutes at Large, 1700–1750. Ed. Waverly K. Winfree. Richmond: Virginia State Library, 1971.
> Ref. K.V471 1700–1750 (also in Mss. and Pub. Docs.)

——. *The Statutes at Large; Being a Collection of All the Laws of Virginia, from the First Session of the Legislature, in the Year 1619.* Ed. William Waller Hening. New York: R. & W. & G. Bartow, 1823; Richmond: Whittet & Shepperson, 1969. 13 vols.
> Ref. K.V471 1619–1792 (1823) 1969 (also in Pub. Docs.)

——. *The Statutes at Large of Virginia, from October Session 1792, to December Session 1806 [i.e., 1807].* Ed. Samuel Shepherd. Richmond: S. Shepherd, 1835–36. 3 vols.
> Ref. K.V471 1792–1808 1835 (also in Pub. Docs.)

The above three works cover the period 1619–1806. They are valuable for land patents, lists of soldiers, and other records of early Virginians. Hening's is indexed in Swem's *Virginia Historical Index.*

Wayland, John Walter. *The German Element of the Shenandoah Valley of Virginia.* Charlottesville, Va.: Michie Book Company, 1907.
> Stacks. F232.S5W3

A brief history of the German element in the Valley, including a bibliography, a listing of some important county records, and an index.

Writers' Program. Virginia. *Virginia: A Guide to the Old Dominion.* New York: Oxford University Press, 1940.
> Ref. F231.W88 1940

Brief histories of Virginia and its major cities. Chiefly a tour guide. Long but dated bibliography on Virginia. Index.

Records

Local court and church records must be searched in any quest for complete genealogical information about a given family. To conduct such a search in Virginia may be difficult because of the confusing changes that have taken place in Virginia's administrative structure since the original eight shires were established in 1634. A large portion of the original territory of Virginia is now in Kentucky and West Virginia. Over the years, counties have been divided, merged, and renamed. The independent city system contributes another complication. For a concise, clear explanation of the counties and cities of Virginia, including dates of creation and extinction, see *The Hornbook of Virginia History.* For outlines of church jurisdiction, see Goodwin, *The Colonial Church in Virginia* and Cocke, *Parish Lines.* The Virginia State Library's *Lists of the Court Records of the Virginia Counties and Cities on Microfilm in the Archives Division* is very useful in searching for records. Microfilm reels of these court records can be ordered through interlibrary loan from the Virginia State Library.

Although it is preferable to go to the original document to discover and verify vital information because of possible errors in transcription, there are many compilations of records of births, deaths, marriages, baptisms, etc., which are helpful to the genealogist. The following is a list of such compilations that are contained in Alderman Library. County and local histories have been omitted from this bibliography. Often these histories have references to local families and even partial or complete genealogies. For a listing of these county histories, see Susan O. Marcell's "Virginia History and Biography: A Guide to Materials in Alderman Library, Including a Bibliography of County Histories" or the subject card catalog under the name of the county or locale (e.g., "Princess Anne County—History").

General Records

Bell, Annie Walker Burns. *Virginia Genealogies and County Records.* Washington, D.C., 1941–   . 11 vols. (See section on Genealogies below.)

Brock, R. A. *Documents, Chiefly Unpublished, Relating to the Huguenot Emigration to Virginia and to the Settlement at Mannakin-Town.* Richmond: Virginia Historical Society, 1886.
Stacks. F221.V82 new ser. v. 5
Includes lists of Huguenot immigrants, especially ship lists, as well as genealogies of selected families. Index.

Clemens, William Montgomery. *Virginia Wills before 1799 . . . Copied from the Court House Records of Amherst, Bedford, Campbell, Loudoun, Prince William, and Rockbridge Counties.* Pompton Lakes, N.J.: The Biblio Company, 1924.

Stacks. F225.C5

Crozier, William Armstrong. *Early Virginia Marriages.* Baltimore: Southern Book Company, 1953.   Ref. F225.C746 1953 Chiefly eighteenth-century marriage records filed in fifteen Virginia counties.

―――. *Virginia County Records.* Hasbrouck Heights, N.J., 1910.

Rare Book Coll. F221.V75

Currer-Briggs, Noel. *Virginia Settlers and English Adventurers: Abstracts of Wills, 1484–1798, and Legal Proceedings, 1560–1700, Relating to Early Virginia Families.* Baltimore: Genealogical Publishing Company, 1970.

Rare Book Coll. F225.C96 1970

DuVall, Lindsay O. *Virginia Colonial Abstracts, Series II.* Washington, D.C., 1951–   .

Rare Book Coll. F225.F58 1937 2d ser. V. 1: Northumberland County, 1678–1713; v. 2: Lancaster County, 1657–80; v. 3: Virginia Company of London, 1607–24; v. 4: James City County, 1634–1904 [*sic*]. An index, with abstracts.

Fleet, Beverley. *Virginia Colonial Abstracts, [First Series].* Richmond, 1937–49.

Ref. F225.F58 1937 1st ser. (also in Rare Book Coll.) V. 1: Lancaster County Record Book No. 2, 1654–66; v. 2: Northumberland County Records, 1652–55; v. 3: Northumberland County Record of Births, 1661–1810; v. 4–7: King and Queen County Records Concerning 18th-Century Persons; v. 8–9: Essex County Wills and Deeds, 1711–14, 1714–17; v. 10–13: Charles City County Court Orders, 1655–58, 1658–61, ·1661–64, 1664–65, Fragments, 1650–96; v. 14–15, 27–28, 33: King and Queen County Records Concerning 18th-Century Persons, 5th–9th Collection. v. 16–17: Richmond County Records, 1692–1704, 1704–

24; v. 18, 32: Acchawmacke, 1632–37, & Accomacke County, 1637–40; v. 19–20: Northumbria Collectanae, 1645–1720; v. 21: Henrico County, Southside, 1736; v. 22: Lancaster County, 1652–55; v. 23: Westmoreland County, 1653–57; v. 24–26: York County, 1653–57, 1646–48, 1648–57; v. 29: Essex County Records, 1703–6; v. 30: Huntington Library Data, 1607–1850; v. 31: Lower Norfolk County, 1651–54; v. 34: Washington County Marriage Register, 1782–1820.

Fothergill, Augusta Bridgland, and John Mark Naugle. *Virginia Tax Payers, 1782–87, Other than Those Published by the United States Census Bureau*. Richmond, 1940.

Rare Book Coll. F225.F6 1940

Greer, George Cabell. *Early Virginia Immigrants, 1623–1666*. Baltimore: Genealogical Publishing Company, 1960.

Ref. F225.G81 1960 (also in Stacks and Rare Book Coll.) Compiled from Land Office records; gives name, date of entry, and sponsor.

Hamlin, Charles Hughes. *They Went Thataway*. Richmond, 1964–66. 3 vols.   Rare Book Coll. F225.H2 1964 Abstracts from Virginia records. Comprehensive personal name index in each volume.

_____. *Virginia: Ancestors and Adventurers*. Richmond, 1967–69. 2 vols.   Rare Book Coll. F225.H24 1967 Abstracts from Virginia court records. Includes Revolutionary War size rolls. Index in each volume.

Hinshaw, William Wade. *Encyclopedia of American Quaker Genealogy*. Ann Arbor, Mich.: Edwards Brothers, 1936–   .

Rare Book Coll. E184.F89H5 1936 Library has only vol. 6, "Virginia." A good compilation of records kept by the Quakers.

Historical Records Survey. Virginia. *Index to Marriage Notices in The Southern Churchman, 1835–1941*. Richmond: The Historical Records Survey of Virginia, 1942.

Stacks. BX5800.S6H5 (also in Mss.)

————. *Inventory of Church Archives of Virginia.* Richmond: The Historical Records Survey of Virginia, 1940–41. 2 vols. in 3.
Stacks. BX6201.R4H5
V. 1: Index to Obituary Notices in *Religious Herald* (Richmond) 1828–1938; v. 2: Index to Marriage Notices in *Religious Herald,* 1828–1938.

Hotten, John Camden. *The Original Lists of Persons of Quality* . . . . (See chapter III.)

Jester, Annie Lash, and Martha Woodroof Hiden. *Adventures of Purse and Person in Virginia, 1607–1625.* Princeton, N.J.: Princeton University Press, 1956.
Ref. CS69.J4 1956 (also in Rare Book Coll.)
Contains the musters of the inhabitants of Virginia, 1624–25, as well as information on those who came to or had land in Virginia during the period 1607–25. Discusses backgrounds and activities of each of these early Virginians and provides much genealogical information.

Nugent, Nell Marion. *Cavaliers and Pioneers: Abstracts of Virginia Land Patents and Grants, 1623–1800.* Richmond: Dietz Printing Company, 1934–   .
Rare Book Coll. F225.N842 1934
Library has vol. 1: 1623–66. Comprehensive index.

Stanard, William Glover. *Some Emigrants to Virginia: Memoranda in Regard to Several Hundred Emigrants to Virginia during the Colonial Period Whose Parentage Is Shown or Former Residence Indicated by Authentic Records.* Richmond: W. E. Jones' Sons, 1911.
Stacks. F229.S81
A compilation from other secondary sources, such as the *Virginia Magazine of History and Biography.* Extensive name index.

Torrence, Clayton. *Virginia Wills and Administrations, 1632–1800: An Index of Wills Recorded in Local Courts of Virginia, 1632–1800, and of Administrations on Estates Shown by Inventories of the Estates of Intestates Recorded in Will (and Other) Books of Local Courts, 1632–1800.* Richmond: The William Byrd Press, 1931.
Ref. F225.T85 1931 (also in Rare Book Coll. and Mss.)

United States Bureau of the Census. *Heads of Families at the First Census of the United States Taken in the Year 1790.* Washington, D.C.: Government Printing Office, 1907–8.

Ref. HA201 1790.C 1907

Lists of heads of families entered in state enumerations in 1782, 1783, 1784, and 1785, used to replace the 1790 federal census records for Virginia, which are missing. Index.

Virginia (Colony) Council. *Legislative Journals of the Council of Colonial Virginia.* Ed. H. R. McIlwaine. Richmond: The Colonial Press, E. Waddey Company, 1918–19. 3 vols.

Rare Book Coll. J87.V6 1680–1773 (also in Pub. Docs.)

_____. *Minutes of the Council and General Court of Colonial Virginia, 1622–1632, 1670–1676.* Ed. H. R. McIlwaine. Richmond: The Colonial Press, E. Waddey Company, 1924.

Rare Book Coll. J87.V612 (also in Rare Book Coll. Typ. V5C6 1924V; and Pub. Docs.)

Indexed.

Virginia (Colony) General Assembly. House of Burgesses. *Journals of the House of Burgesses of Virginia, 1619–[1776].* Richmond: The Colonial Press, E. Waddey Company, 1905–15. 13 vols. Pub. Docs. (Mss. has on microfilm)

The above three works are compilations of colonial Virginia records that offer many references to colonial Virginians.

Virginia Company of London. *The Records of the Virginia Company of London.* Ed. Susan Myra Kingsbury. Washington, D.C.: Government Printing Office, 1906–35. 4 vols.

Stacks. F229.V86 1906 (also in Rare Book Coll.; v. 1–2 in Ref.)

V. 1–2: Court book, 1619–24, index in v. 2; v. 3–4: Documents.

Virginia County Records . . . . New York: The Genealogical Association, 1905–13. 11 vols.   Rare Book Coll. F221.V75

Holdings of Alderman Library: v. 1: Spotsylvania County, 1721–1800 (also in stacks); v. 2: Virginia Colonial Militia, 1651–1776 (also in Ref.); v. 5: Virginia Heraldica (also in Ref. and stacks); v. 6–7: Virginia County Records (also in stacks); v. 8: A Key to Southern Pedigrees (also in Ref.);

v. 9–10: Virginia County Records and Heraldic Quarterly Register of the United States and Canada.

Waldenmaier, Inez. *A Finding List of Virginia Marriage Records before 1853*. Washington, D.C., 1957.
Rare Book Coll. F225.W16 1957

Worrell, Anne Lowry. *Over the Mountain Men: Their Early Court Records in Southwest Virginia*. Baltimore, Md.: Genealogical Publishing Co., 1962.
Rare Book Coll. F225.W67 1962 (also in Stacks. F225.W67 1934)

Wulfeck, Dorothy Ford. *Marriages of Some Virginia Residents, 1607–1800*. Naugatuck, Conn., 1961–67. 7 vols.
Rare Book Coll. F225.W7 1961

Militia Lists
Colonial and Revolutionary Lists

Brumbaugh, Gaius Marcus. *Revolutionary War Records*. Washington, D.C., 1936– .   Rare Book Coll. E255.B85
Library has vol. 1: Virginia. Includes lists of officers and noncommissioned officers who served in the Virginia army and navy, regimental lists, and lists of bounty land applicants. Comprehensive index.

Burgess, Louis Alexander. *Virginia Soldiers of 1776*. Richmond: Richmond Press, 1927–29; Spartanburg, S.C.: Reprint Company, 1973. 3 vols.
Stacks. E263.V8B9 1973 (also in Mss.)
Compiled from the land bounties filed in the Virginia Land Office for land grants issued in Kentucky and Ohio as reward for military service in the Revolutionary War. The claims of heirs as well as soldiers are listed; therefore some family relationships can be traced. Index for vols. 1–2 in vol. 2, for vol. 3 in vol. 3.

Crozier, William Armstrong. *Virginia Colonial Militia, 1651–1776*. Baltimore: Southern Book Company, 1954.
Ref. F221.V75 v.2 1954 (also in Rare Book Coll. and Stacks)

Regiment rosters, land bounty certificate lists, militia officers, and miscellaneous lists of militia men serving in the wars from 1651 to 1776. Comprehensive index.

Daughters of the American Revolution. Virginia. *Roster of the Virginia Daughters of the American Revolution (Revised), 1890–1958*. Richmond: Garrett & Massie, 1959.

> Ref. E202.5.V87 1959 (also in Stacks)

Part 1: list of members of the Virginia chapter of the DAR, with reference to each member's patriot ancestor(s). Part 2: list of ancestors officially recognized by the DAR as patriots. Each entry includes the patriot's birth and death dates; place, date, and rank of Revolutionary service; and reference to DAR members.

Dorman, John Frederick. *Virginia Revolutionary Pension Applications*. Washington, D.C., 1958–64. 9 vols.

> Rare Book Coll. E263.V8D6 1958

Abstracts of Revolutionary War pension applications. Information includes name of soldier, summary of service, list of supportive documents registered with the applications, and number and date of certificate issued. Index in each volume.

Gwathmey, John Hastings. *Historical Register of Virginians in the Revolution: Soldiers, Sailors, Marines, 1775–1783*. Richmond: Dietz Press, 1938.

> Ref. E263.V8G9 (also in Rare Book Coll.)

Briefly identifies each soldier and gives the source of the service record. Key to sources: p. xiii.

McAllister, Joseph Thompson. *Virginia Militia in the Revolutionary War*. Hot Springs, Va.: McAllister Publishing Company, 1913.

> Ref. E263.V8M13

Describes the services of each company in the war. List of officers, by county; lists of pensioners. Index.

_____. *Index to Saffell's List of Virginia Soldiers in the Revolution*. Hot Springs, Va.. McAllister Publishing Company, 1913.

> Ref. E263.V8M11 1913

Index to the Virginia records portion of William Saffell's *Records of the Revolutionary War*.

McGhee, Lucy Kate Walker. *Virginia Pension Abstracts of the Wars of the Revolution, 1812, and Indian Wars.* Washington, D.C., 1957?–66. 35 vols.
　　　　　　　　　　Rare Book Coll. E359.5.V8M23 1957
Abstracts of pension applications, including supportive depositions. Information about the family usually included. Index in each volume.

Stewart, Robert Armistead. *The History of Virginia's Navy of the Revolution.* Richmond: Mitchell & Hotchkiss, 1933.
　　　　　　　　　　Stacks. F230.S84 1933
"Roster of the Virginia Navy of the Revolution": pp. 187–271.

Torrence, Clayton. *Genealogy of Members, Sons of Revolution in the State of Virginia.* Richmond: Mitchell & Hotchkiss, 1939.
　　　　　　　　　　Ref. F225.T84 (also in Rare Book Coll.)
Genealogies of colonial and revolutionary Virginians.

Virginia. Commissioner of Revolutionary Claims. *A List of Officers of the Army and Navy, Who Have Received Lands from Virginia for Revolutionary Services, the Quantity Received, When Received, the Time of Service for Which Each Officer Received Land, &c., Down to September, 1833.* Virginia. General Assembly, 1833/34, House Doc. 30. Richmond, 1833.
　　　　　　　　　　Rare Book Coll. E263.V8V5 1833
Extracted from documents accompanying Virginia General Assembly, House of Delegates, Journal, 1833/34. Lists name of soldier, rank, line and time of service, number of acres granted, and date of warrant.

———. *A List of That Portion of Armand's Corps . . . Entitled to Land from the United States, and from Virginia, &c.; A List of Soldiers, (Virginians) Who Were Reported . . . as Not Having Claimed Their Warrants for Bounty Land . . . on File in the Bounty Land Office January 16th, 1828; A List of Soldiers (of the Invalid Regiment . . .) Who Were Reported . . . 18th January, 1828, Entitled to Bounty Land from the United States; A List of Officers and Soldiers of the Virginia Continental Line . . . Entitled to Bounty Land . . . ; A List of Officers and Soldiers,*

Who Have Been Allowed Bounty Land by the Executive of Virginia, and Who Have Not Received Warrants Therefor; A List of Non-commissioned Officers and Soldiers . . . Entitled to Bounty Land from Virginia. Virginia. General Assembly, 1833/34, House Doc. 34. Richmond, 1833.

Rare Book Coll. E263.V8V52 1833

Lists name and rank; some lists include service dates and line.

Virginia. State Library. Dept. of Archives and History. *List of the Colonial Soldiers of Virginia: Special Report of the Department of Archives and History for 1913.* H. J. Eckenrode, Archivist. Richmond: D. Bottom, Superintendent of Public Printing, 1917.

Ref. F229.V94 1917 (also in Pub. Docs.)

_____. *List of the Revolutionary Soldiers of Virginia: Special Report of the Department of Archives and History for 1911.* H. J. Eckenrode, Archivist. Richmond: D. Bottom, Superintendent of Public Printing, 1912.

Rare Book Coll. E263.V8V79 (also in Pub. Docs.)

Alphabetical list of Virginia Revolutionary soldiers with reference to original document sources in each entry. Key to sources: pp. 12–13.

Wilson, Samuel M. *Catalogue of Revolutionary Soldiers and Sailors of the Commonwealth of Virginia to Whom Land Bounty Warrants Were Granted by Virginia for Military Services in the War for Independence.* Baltimore: Southern Book Company, 1953.

Ref. E263.V8W5 1953 (also in Rare Book Coll.)

Includes date of warrant and amount of land given.

War of 1812

McGhee, Lucy Kate Walker. *Virginia Pension Abstracts of the Wars of the Revolution, 1812, and Indian Wars.* (See preceding section.)

Sweeney, Lenora Elizabeth. "Orderly Book, Virginia Militia, War of 1812," *Virginia Magazine of History and Biography* 46 (1938): 246–53, 329–38.

Ref. F221.V91 (also in Stacks)

Virginia. Auditor's Office. *Muster Rolls of the Virginia Militia in the War of 1812; Being a Supplement to the Pay Rolls Printed and Distributed in 1851.* Richmond: W. F. Ritchie, 1852.
Rare Book Coll. F359.5.V8V81
Supplement to the following work.

——. *Pay Rolls of Militia Entitled to Land Bounty under the Act of Congress of Sept. 28, 1850.* Richmond: W. F. Ritchie, 1851.
Ref. E359.5.V8V8 1851 (also in Rare Book Coll.)
Payrolls of Virginia militia entered at the Auditor's Office. No index.

Civil War

Manarin, Louis Henry, and Lee A. Wallace, Jr. *Richmond Volunteers: The Volunteer Companies of the City of Richmond and Henrico County, Virginia, 1861–1865.* Richmond: Westover Press, 1970.
Rare Book Coll. F234.R5M3 1970

Genealogies

This is a selective list of some of the more important Virginia genealogies in Alderman Library. Most of the works listed are collective genealogies. To ascertain whether or not the library has a printed genealogy of a specific family, look in the subject card catalog under the family name (e.g., "Walker Family"). The Library of Congress bibliography of genealogies (see chapter I); Brown, *Virginia Genealogies;* and Stewart, *Index to Printed Virginia Genealogies* should be consulted for genealogies of specific families contained in larger works held in Alderman Library.

Ackerly, Mary Denham, and L. E. J. Parker. *Our Kin: The Genealogies of Some of the Early Families Who Made History in the Founding and Development of Bedford County, Virginia.* Lynchburg, Va.: J. P. Bell Company, 1930.
Rare Book Coll. F232.B4A17 1930
Refers to families in Bedford and Campbell counties.

Bell, Annie Walker Burns. *Virginia Genealogies and County Records.* Washington, D.C., 1941–   . 11 vols.
Rare Book Coll. F225.B38

Includes family records, census reports, wills, pension abstracts, etc. No index.

Boddie, John Bennett. *Historical Southern Families.* (See chapter III.)

_____. *Southside Virginia Families.* Redwood City, Calif.: Pacific Coast Publishers, 1955.
> Rare Book Coll. F225.B6 1955

Genealogies of selected families. Comprehensive personal name index.

_____. *Virginia Historical Genealogies.* Redwood City, Calif.: Pacific Coast Publishers, 1954.
> Rare Book Coll. F225.B64 1954

Genealogies of selected families. Comprehensive name index.

Brock, R. A. *Documents, Chiefly Unpublished, Relating to the Huguenot Emigration of Virginia . . . .* (See section on Records, General, above.)

Brown, Alexander. *The Cabells and Their Kin.* 2d ed. Richmond: Garrett & Massie, 1939.
> Stacks. CS71.C11 1939 (1895 ed. also in Stacks)

Amherst, Buckingham, and Nelson county families.

Conway, Moncure Daniel. *Barons of the Potomack and the Rappahannock.* New York: The Grolier Club, 1892.
> Stacks. F225.C67 (also Rare Book Coll. Typ. 1892.C65)

A miscellaneous collection of letters of prominent early Virginians, especially relating to the Washington and Lewis families.

Donaldson, Evelyn Kinder. *Squires and Dames of Old Virginia.* Los Angeles: Miller Printing Company, 1950.
> Rare Book Coll. CS71.W34

Genealogy and records of the Watson family.

Foley, Louise Pledge Heath. *Early Virginia Families along the James River: Their Deep Roots and Tangled Branches.* Richmond: Foley, 1974–78. 2 vols.   Stacks F225.F596

Data on Henrico, Charles City, Goochland, and Prince George counties.

Goode, George Brown. *Virginia Cousins: A Study of the Ancestry and Posterity of John Goode of Whitby.* Bridgewater, Va.: C. J. Carrier, 1963.
> Stacks. CS71.G647 (also in Rare Book Coll.)
Traces the Goode family from England to America. Notes on other English Goodes. Index.

Hayden, Horace Edwin. *Virginia Genealogies.* Washington, D.C.: The Rare Book Shop, 1931.   Ref. F225.H41 1931
Genealogies of the following Virginia families: Glassell, Ball, Brown, Bryan, Conway, Daniel, Ewell, Holladay, Lewis, Littlepage, Moncure, Peyton, Robinson, Scott, Taylor, Wallace. Comprehensive name index. Also indexed in Stewart's *Index to Printed Virginia Genealogies.*

Kennedy, Mary Selden. *Seldens of Virginia and Allied Families.* New York: Frank Allaben Genealogical Company, 1911.
> Ref. CS71.S458 1911
An extensive genealogy of the descendants of Samuel and Rebecca Yeo Selden. Includes coats of arms. Index.

Lester, Memory Lee Alldredge. *Bible Records.* Chapel Hill, N.C., 1956–62. 7 vols.   Rare Book Coll. CS69.L4 1956
Southern Bible records, many of which are not in print elsewhere.

McIlhany, Hugh Milton. *Some Virginia Families; Being Genealogies of the Kinney, Stribling, Trout, McIlhany, Milton, Rogers, Tate, Snickers, Taylor, McCormick, and Other Families of Virginia.* Staunton, Va.: Stoneburner & Prufer, Printers, 1903.
> Rare Book Coll. F225.M15 1903

National Society of the Colonial Dames of America. Virginia. *History and Register of Ancestors and Members of the Society . . . , 1892–1930.* Richmond: The William Byrd Press, 1930.
> Stacks. E186.4.V84 1930

Norford, William Lindsay. *Norford Family History, 1742–1965.* Charlottesville, Va.: The Michie Company, 1965.
> Stacks. CS71.N928 1965

Eight generations of Virginia Norfords. Appendixes: Norford family documents.

Oliver, Lloyd F. *Index to Du Bellet's* Some Prominent Virginia Families. Tomball, Tex.: Genealogical Publications, 1979.
Ref. F225.043
Separately published index to Pecquet du Bellet (below).

Pecquet du Bellet, Louise. *Some Prominent Virginia Families.* Lynchburg, Va.: J. P. Bell, 1907.   Ref. F225.P36
Selected families traced. Indexed by Oliver (above).

Robertson, Wyndham, and R. A. Brock. *Pocahontas, Alias Matoaka, and Her Descendants.* Richmond: J. W. Randolph & English, 1887. Reprint, 1932.
Ref. CS71.R747 1887 1932 ed.
Includes some brief biographical sketches and portraits.

Selden, Edna Mae. *Selden and Kindred of Virginia.* Richmond: Virginia Stationery Company, 1941.
Stacks. CS71.S458 1941
Not as extensive as Kennedy's book (above). Index.

Valentine, Edward Pleasants. *The Edward Pleasants Valentine Papers: Abstracts of Records in the Local and General Archives of Virginia Relating to the Families of Allen, Bacon, Ballard, Batchelder, Blouet, Brassieur (Brashear), Cary, Crenshaw, Dabney, Exum, Ferris, Fontaine, Gray, Hardy, Isham (Henrico County), Jordan, Langston, Lyddall, Mann, Mosby, Palmer, Pasteur, Pleasants, Povall, Randolph, Satterwhite, Scott, Smith (the Family of Francis Smith of Hanover County), Valentine, Waddy, Watts, Winston, Womack, Woodson.* Richmond: The Valentine Museum, 1927.
Ref. F225.V17 (also in Stacks and Rare Book Coll.)
Abstracts of wills, deeds, and court orders collected by Edward Pleasants Valentine relating to the above families.

Van Meter, Benjamin Franklin. *Genealogies and Sketches of Some Old Families Who Have Taken Prominent Part in the Development of Virginia and Kentucky . . . .* Louisville, Ky.: J. P. Morton & Company, 1901.   Stacks. F450.V26 1901

Lewis, Phillips, Moss, Van Meter, Cunningham, Harness families; J. H. McNeill and his rangers.

Manuscript Sources

The Manuscripts Department has vital records, family papers, and a few genealogies which may be of use to the genealogist. Most of these records concern Virginians, especially those who lived in Charlottesville and Albemarle County. The Manuscripts Department maintains its own card catalog in the Manuscripts Reading Room; Alderman's main card catalog does not contain manuscript holdings.

The following Manuscripts Department holdings can prove fruitful in genealogical research.

Virginia Census.

Original census records (1790 to present) for Virginia only are kept on microfilm produced by the National Archives. Indexes to census records have been compiled by various individuals and organizations (most recently by Accelerated Indexing Systems, Inc., of Bountiful, Utah, which apparently plans to generate them for all the states); to find the one you are seeking, consult the subject card catalog under the name of the state and the requisite census (e.g., "Virginia—Census 1810—Indexes").

Bible Records.

The Manuscripts Department photocopies family record pages from Bibles as they are acquired and keeps the copies in a vertical file arranged alphabetically by family name. An index to these records, Bayne Palmer O'Brien's "Bible Records of Virginia Families in the Manuscripts Division, Alderman Library, University of Virginia," *The Virginia Genealogist* 15 (1971): 206–11, is kept in the file for easy reference.

Family Papers.

Although the holdings of the Manuscripts Department are voluminous, it is difficult to glean genealogical information from the family papers housed there. Because of the handwriting and condition of the papers, a great deal of time can be expended in reading through letters and other manuscripts, and it is possible that there will be few, if any, references of use to the genealogist. All family papers are indexed in the Manuscripts subject card catalog.

Albemarle County Wills and Deeds.
The records of wills and deeds filed in Albemarle County from the 1700s to the 1920s, microfilmed by the Virginia State Library.

Charlottesville and Albemarle County Cemetery Records.
The local chapter of the Daughters of the American Revolution has compiled a list of those buried in most of the area cemeteries. At this time, these records are not totally inclusive, as some of the municipal cemeteries have not yet been surveyed; however, the DAR is continuing this project and keeping the list updated.

Special Genealogical Collections.
McClenney Collection.
Typescripts of genealogical histories of Nansemond County.

McKay Genealogy.
The working papers for an extensive genealogy of the McKay family are kept with bound indexes to the material covered.

Herndon Collection.
Genealogies of the Herndon and related families.

Guides.
Virginia. University. Library. *Report on Historical Collections.* Charlottesville, Va., 1930–50.
Ref. CD3560.V5 (also in Stacks)
A subject guide to manuscripts in the Alderman Library collection. Each entry includes a description of the manuscripts and accession numbers. Index appears in the front of each bound volume.

_____. Manuscripts Department. *Monthly News Notes.* Charlottesville, Va., 1955– .
Rare Book Coll. Z6620.U5V5 (also in Mss.)

Monthly list of new acquisitions to Alderman's manuscripts collection, with brief descriptions and accession numbers.

Homes and Houses

At some point in the genealogical investigation, a search for information on houses may prove fruitful. Any history of a house should include at least a listing of owners, and many have interesting anecdotes revealing some aspects of the lives and personalities of the owners. Below are listed the main sources on Virginia houses in Alderman Library. For additional books, consult the subject card catalog under the name of the city or county (e.g., "Princess Anne County—Historic houses, etc.") or under "Virginia—Description."

Farrar, Emmie Ferguson. *Old Virginia Houses.* New York: Hastings House, 1955–   .
> Ref. E227.F3 (also in Rare Book Coll. and Fine Arts)
> Short histories and descriptions of a large number of houses, with many photographs of exteriors, some interiors. Index includes names of owners. Contents: v. 1. The Mobjack Bay Country; v. 2. Along the James; v. 3. Along the Fall Line; v. 4. The Northern Peninsulas; v. 5. The Heart of Virginia.

Garden Club of Virginia. *Homes and Gardens in Old Virginia.* Ed. Susanne Williams Massie and Frances Archer Christian. Richmond: Garrett & Massie, 1950.
> Ref. SB466.U7V8 1950 (also in Rare Book Coll., Fine Arts, and Sci. Tech.)
> Arranged by location; gives brief history and description of major estates with emphasis on trees and gardens. Photographs of exteriors. Index.

Lancaster, Robert A., Jr. *Historic Virginia Homes and Churches.* Philadelphia: J. B. Lippincott, 1915.
> Ref. F227.L24 (also in Rare Book Coll., Fine Arts, and Stacks)
> Covering colonial Virginia homes of historic interest, this work emphasizes descriptions of the occupants rather than architecture. Small photographs of most of the houses are included. Index of names.

Mead, Edward C. *Historic Homes of the South-West Mountains, Virginia*. Philadelphia: J. B. Lippincott, 1899.
Ref. F232.A3M4 1899 (also in Rare Book Coll. and Stacks)
Detailed descriptions of twenty-eight of Albemarle County's historic homes and their families. No index.

National Trust for Historic Preservation in the United States. *Virginia Inventory*. 1960– .   Mss.
Sites of national and statewide significance are included in this survey. Photographs and historical data are given.

Nutting, Wallace. *Virginia Beautiful*. Garden City, N.Y.: Garden City Pub. Co., 1930.
Stacks. F231.N98 (also in Rare Book Coll. and Fine Arts)
Unique among Virginia house books in emphasis on architectural details and, although very selective, worth consulting for this aspect.

Rawlings, Mary. *Ante-bellum Albemarle*. (See next section.)

Rothery, Agnes. *Houses Virginians Have Loved*. New York: Rinehart & Co., 1954.
Ref. NA7235.V5R6 1954 (also in Rare Book Coll. and Stacks)
About 100 lesser-known Virginia houses described with emphasis on personal incidents involved with the houses rather than architectural details.

Sale, Edith Tunis. *Interiors of Virginia Houses of Colonial Times*. Richmond: William Byrd Press, 1927.
Rare Book Coll. NA7235.V5S3 (also in Fine Arts)
Excellent descriptive details, room by room, of major colonial houses, interspersed with family history. Photographs of exteriors and interiors and floor plans. Index.

Stevens, William T. *Virginia House Tour*. Charlottesville, Va.: William T. Stevens, 1962.
Ref. F227.S89 (also in Rare Book Coll., Fine Arts, and Stacks)
Concentrating on Albemarle County and the surrounding area, giving brief history and description. Many photographs.

Virginia Vertical File (Reference Dept.)
A collection of newspaper clippings from the Charlottesville *Daily Progress* and Richmond *Times Dispatch,* brochures, and miscellaneous information. Kept in the filing cabinets near the reference desk. The coverage is generally limited to Charlottesville and adjacent counties.

Wayland, John Walter. *Historic Homes of Northern Virginia and the Eastern Panhandle of West Virginia.* Staunton, Va.: The McClure Co., 1937.
Ref. F227.W38 (also in Rare Book Coll.)
One of the more rewarding house books, this gives a fairly detailed history of each house and its inhabitants with numerous photographs of exteriors, interiors, and grounds. Maps show exact location of houses. Good index.

Charlottesville and Albemarle County

"Albemarle County Marriages," *Virginia Magazine of History and Biography* 31 (1923): 333–38, 32 (1924): 365–69.
Ref. F221.V91 (also in Stacks and Mss.)
The marriage book of Rev. John Gibson of Albemarle County. Lists marriages (name of groom and bride) chronologically.

Alexander, James. *Early Charlottesville: Recollections of James Alexander, 1828–1874.* Ed. Mary Rawlings. Charlottesville, Va.: Albemarle County Historical Society, 1963.
Ref. F234.C4A4 1942 1963 ed. (also in Rare Book Coll., Mss., and Stacks)
Reminiscences of newspaper editor and longtime Charlottesville resident James Alexander. Provides descriptions of families, houses, and streets of Charlottesville during the period 1828–74. Index.

Coddington, Anne Bartlett, and Edward N. Dunlap. *A Genealogical Index to the* History of Albemarle County, Virginia. Philadelphia: Magee Press, 1936.   Ref. F232.A3W83 1936
Indexes Woods (below).

Dabney, William Minor. "Jefferson's Albemarle: History of Albemarle County, Virginia, 1727–1819." Ph.D. diss., University of Virginia, 1951.
Ref. University of Virginia Dissertation 637 (also in Rare Book Coll.)
A history and description of early Albemarle County, including the Revolutionary period. Topics covered include settlers, the justice system and courts, agriculture, education, medicine, slavery, labor, travel, towns and taverns, religious and social life, business, and politics. Bibliography; no index.

Hemphill, W. Edwin, and Evelyn Dollens. "Marriages in Albemarle County, 1780–1785," *Papers of the Albemarle County Historical Society* 6 (1945–46): 41–62.
Ref. F232.A3M3 (also in Rare Book Coll. and Stacks)
Two compilations of Albemarle County marriage records for the period 1780–85. Comprehensive index includes names of grooms, brides, and sureties.

Jones, Newton Bond. "Charlottesville and Albemarle County, Virginia, 1819–1860." Ph.D. diss., University of Virginia, 1950.
Ref. University of Virginia Dissertation 602 (also in Rare Book Coll.)
Similar to Dabney's study above, this work covers the periods 1819–29 and 1850–60. Bibliography; no index.

King, Junie Estelle Stewart. *Abstracts of Wills, Inventories, and Administration Accounts of Albemarle County, Virginia, 1748–1800*. Beverly Hills, Calif., 1964.
Ref. F232.A3K45 1940 (also in Rare Book Coll.)
Brief abstracts of Albemarle County will books A, B (2), 3, and 4 (i.e., 1748–1800). List of wills, 1800–1804, without abstracts. List of pensions to 1835; list of inventories, 1749–1800. Index by surname only.

Magazine of Albemarle County History. Charlottesville, Va., 1940– .
Ref. F232.A3M3 (also in Rare Book Coll. and Stacks)
Formerly *Papers of the Albemarle County Historical Society*, this

annual journal publishes articles of local historical interest. Indexed vols. 1–20.

Moore, John Hammond. *Albemarle: Jefferson's County, 1727–1976.* Charlottesville, Va.: University Press of Virginia, 1976.
 Ref. F232.A3M66 (also in Stacks, Mss., and Fine Arts)

Murphy, Mary Catharine. "Abstracts of Marriages in Charlottesville Newspapers, 1820–1859," *Magazine of Albemarle County History* 21 (1962–63): 23–53.
 Ref. F232.A3M3 (also in Rare Book Coll. and Stacks) Abstracts of marriage announcements from the Charlottesville newspapers *The Central Gazette, Virginia Advocate,* and *Jeffersonian Republican.*

————. "Abstracts of Obituaries in Charlottesville Newspapers, 1860–1869," *Magazine of Albemarle County History* 23 (1964–65): 45–70.
 Ref. F232.A3M3 (also in Rare Book Coll. and Stacks) Abstracts of obituaries from the Charlottesville newspapers *Virginia Advocate, Jeffersonian Republican, Daily Chronicle, Tri-Weekly Chronicle, Semi-Weekly Chronicle,* and the *Charlottesville Chronicle.*

————. "Abstracts of Obituaries in Charlottesville Newspapers, 1827–1859," *Magazine of Albemarle County History* 19 (1960–61): 41–57.
 Ref. F232.A3M3 (also in Rare Book Coll. and Stacks) Abstracts of obituaries from the Charlottesville newspapers *The Central Gazette, Virginia Advocate,* and *Jeffersonian Republican.*

————. "Guardians' Bonds of Albemarle County, Virginia, 1783–1852." Typescript. Charlottesville, Va., 1968.
 Rare Book Coll. F232.A3M8 1968 (also in Mss.) Abstracts of guardians' bonds, listing name of orphan, parent, guardian, security, date, amount of bond, and page on which the record is located in the county guardian books. Section I: loose bonds, 1783–1824; Section II: bonds from the county bond book, 1829–44; Section III: bond book, 1844–52. Comprehensive index.

Norford, William L. *Marriages of Albemarle County and Charlottes-ville, Virginia, 1781–1929*. Charlottesville, Va.: Jarman Print-ing Company, 1956.
Ref. F232.A3N6 1956 (also in Rare Book Coll. and Mss.) Lists Albemarle County marriages for 1781–1929 and Char-lottesville marriages for 1888–1929. Arranged alphabetically by groom's surname and chronologically within each letter of the alphabet. No index.

Rachal, William, ed. "Marriage Notices from *The Central Gazette, 1820–1827,*" *Virginia Magazine of History and Biography* 62 (1954): 124–31.
Ref. F221.V91 (also in Stacks and Mss.) Abstracts of marriages recorded in Charlottesville's first newspaper, the weekly *Central Gazette.*

____. "Obituaries from *The Central Gazette,* 1820–1827," *Papers of the Albemarle County Historical Society* 10 (1949–50): 31–38.
Ref. F232.A3M3 (also in Rare Book Coll. and Stacks) Abstracts of obituaries from *The Central Gazette* issues in Alderman Library.

Rawlings, Mary. *The Albemarle of Other Days*. Charlottesville, Va.: The Michie Company, 1925.
Ref. F232.A3R2 (also in Stacks and Rare Book Coll.) A history of Albemarle County, emphasizing Jefferson's life-time. Includes early Albemarle map. Index.

____. *Ante-bellum Albemarle*. Charlottesville, Va.: Peoples Na-tional Bank, 1935.
Ref. F232.A3R17 1935 (also in Stacks and Rare Book Coll.) Brief historical sketches of local buildings and estates, includ-ing ownership history. Index.

Richey, Homer. *Memorial of the John Bowie Strange Camp, United Confederate Veterans*. Charlottesville, Va.: The Michie Com-pany, 1920.   Stacks. E483.1.V5R5
Includes biographical sketches of soldiers from Albemarle County who served in the Confederate army.

St. Claire, Emily Entwisle. *Beautiful and Historic Albemarle.* Richmond: Appeals Press, 1932.
    Ref. F232.A3S3 1932 (also in Rare Book Coll. and Mss.)
    Historical sketch of Albemarle County and Charlottesville. Index not all-inclusive.

Walker's Parish, Albemarle County, Virginia. "Record of Marriages from the Parish Register, Walker's Parish, Albemarle County, Va., from 1885 to 1956." Ed. Susan Metcalfe Musselman. Typescript. 1958.
                            Rare Book Coll. F232.A3W2 1958

Watts, Charles Wilder. "Colonial Albemarle: The Social and Economic History of a Piedmont Virginia County, 1727–1775." M.A. thesis, University of Virginia, 1948.
    Ref. University of Virginia Master's Thesis 1507 (also in Rare Book Coll.)
    Discusses land settlement, patents, and speculation, as well as the economic, social, religious, and educational aspects of the time. Appendix III, pp. 110–79: chronological list of land patents in Albemarle County through 1774. Map shows locations of land for the patents granted.

Webb, William Edward. "Charlottesville and Albemarle County, Virginia, 1865–1900." Ph.D. diss., University of Virginia, 1955.
    Ref. University of Virginia Dissertation 805 (also in Rare Book Coll.)
    A social, economic, and political survey. Bibliography; no index.

Woods, Edgar. *Albemarle County in Virginia.* Charlottesville, Va.: The Michie Company, 1901.
    Ref. F232.A3W8 1901 (also in Stacks, Rare Book Coll., and Mss.)
    A history of Albemarle County. Appendixes give miscellaneous lists of people (such as soldiers, county officials, legislators) and a necrology. Indexed by Coddington (above).

Writers' Program. Virginia. *Jefferson's Albemarle: A Guide to Albemarle County and the City of Charlottesville, Virginia.* Charlottesville, Va.: Jarman's, 1941.

Ref. F232.A3W87 (also in Stacks, Rare Book Coll., and Mss.)
Chiefly a tour guide, with some historical references. Index.

Wyllie, Evelyn Dollens. "Marriage Bonds in Albemarle County, 1786–1795," *Papers of the Albemarle County Historical Society* 9 (1948–49): 42–75.
Ref. F232.A3M3 (also in Rare Book Coll. and Stacks)
A continuation of Hemphill and Dollens above. Comprehensive index.

University of Virginia

Patrons interested in genealogical research involving University of Virginia alumni will find a variety of helpful sources in Alderman Library.

The Reference Department has a complete collection of University of Virginia catalogs and student directories. A vertical file of material related to all aspects of the university's history, including biographical material on past and present faculty members, noteworthy alumni and students, and student organizations, is available in the Reference Office. The university newspapers, *College Topics* and *The Cavalier Daily,* the *Alumni News,* and the *Alumni Bulletin* are also available in the Reference Room. There is an incomplete index to the *Alumni News* and the *Alumni Bulletin* available for patron use. The *Cavalier Daily* index, begun in the 1890s, is shelved behind the Reference Desk and is available for patrons.

The Manuscripts Department has the University Matriculation Books, as well as the minutes of the Faculty and the Board of Visitors. These manuscript sources can be extremely helpful in locating biographical information on university alumni.

The following list of sources should be consulted first in order to verify enrollment.

Schele de Vere, Maximilian. *Students of the University of Virginia.* Baltimore: Charles Harvey & Co., 1878.
Ref. LD5675.3 1878 (also in Rare Book Coll., Mss., and Stacks)
A listing, in alphabetical order, of students who matriculated at the university from the first session in 1825 to 1875. Bi-

ographical information includes date of matriculation, occupation, and death date (if known).

University of Virginia: Its History, Influence, Equipment, and Characteristics with Biographical Sketches and Portraits of Founders, Benefactors, Officers, and Alumni. New York: Lewis Publishing Company, 1904. 2 vols.   Ref. LD5678.B2 1904
The last half of volume I and all of volume II are devoted to biographical sketches. There is a name index to both volumes following the title page of volume II.

Virginia. University. Alumni Association. *Directory of the Living Alumni of the University of Virginia.* Ed. Lewis D. Crenshaw. Charlottesville: University of Virginia Press, 1921.
Ref. LD5675.3 1921 (also in Rare Book Coll. and Stacks)
An alphabetical, geographical, and class year index of the living alumni of the university from the Class of 1845 to the Class of 1920. Brief biographical information is noted when available.

_____. *Directory of the Living Alumni of the University of Virginia.* Charlottesville, Va.: The Michie Company, 1931.
Ref. LD5675.3 1931 (also in Mss., Stacks, and Rare Book Coll.)
Updates the *Directory* above through the class of 1930.

_____. *Alumni Directory, 1981.* White Plains, N.Y.: Bernard C. Harris, 1981.   Ref. LD5675.3 1981
Lists living alumni from the Class of 1900 to the Class of 1980.

_____. Colonnade Club. *Alphabetical List of Alumni of the University of Virginia.* Charlottesville, Va.: Colonnade Club, 1910.
Ref. LD5675.3 1910 (also in Rare Book Coll. and Stacks)
List of names and addresses of alumni whose whereabouts were known in 1910. Members of the Colonnade Club are noted.

_____. Law School Association. *Directory of Alumni of the Law School, the University of Virginia, 1962.* Charlottesville, Va.: The Michie Company, 1963.

Ref. LD5675.3 1963 (also in Stacks and Law Library)
An alphabetical listing of all the alumni of the School of Law
from the first class in 1826 through the Class of 1962.

____. *Directory of Alumni of the Law School, the University of Virginia, 1972.* Charlottesville, Va.: The Michie Company, 1972.   Law Library. VL163.A47 1972
Updates School of Law alumni through the Class of 1972.

____. Medical Alumni Association. *Directory.* Charlottesville, 1917– .
Ref. R747.V88 (also in Rare Book Coll. and Health Sci.)
Issued periodically (1917, '51, '52, '55, '58, '62, '67), the
directory contains an alphabetical list of the members of the
association with addresses and a geographical list arranged by
state and city. Medical specialities are noted.

AUTHOR-TITLE INDEX